Gonigle
venue
n
20 1HX

D1100924

What a Time to Be Wesleyan!

Other Books by David L. McKenna:

The Urban Crisis (1968)

Awake, My Conscience (1977) (reprinted as
   Contemporary Issues for Evangelical Christians)

The Jesus Model (1978)

The Communicator's Commentary: Mark (1982)

MegaTruth: The Church in the Age of Information (1986)

*Power to Follow; Grace to Lead: Strategy for the Future of
   Christian Leadership* (1986)

The Communicator's Commentary: Job (1986)

Renewing Our Ministry (1986)

The Whisper of His Grace (1987)

Discovering Job (1989)

Love Your Work (1989)

The Coming Great Awakening (1990)

When Our Parents Need Us Most (1994)

The Communicator's Commentary: Isaiah 1—39 (1994)

The Communicator's Commentary: Isaiah 40—66 (1994)

*A Future with a History: The Wesleyan Witness of the Free
   Methodist Church* (1997)

Growing Up in Christ (1998)

Journey Through a Bypass: The Story of an Open Heart
   (1998)

What a Time to Be Wesleyan!

Proclaiming the Holiness Message with Passion and Purpose

David L. McKenna

Beacon Hill Press of Kansas City
Kansas City, Missouri

Copyright 1999
by Beacon Hill Press of Kansas City

ISBN 083-411-769X

Printed in the United States of America

Cover Design: Kevin Williamson

Permission to quote from the following copyrighted versions of the Bible is acknowledged with appreciation:

Unless otherwise indicated, Scripture quotations are from the *Holy Bible, New International Version®* (NIV®). Copyright © 1973, 1978, 1984 by International Bible Society. Used by permission of Zondervan Publishing House. All rights reserved.

Scripture marked KJV is from the King James Version.

Scripture marked NEB is from the *New English Bible* (NEB). Copyright © by the Delegates of the Oxford University Press and the Syndics of the Cambridge University Press, 1961, 1970. Reprinted by permission.

Scripture marked NKJV is from the *New King James Version* (NKJV). Copyright © 1979, 1980, 1982 Thomas Nelson, Inc.

Scripture marked NRSV is from the *New Revised Standard Version* (NRSV) of the Bible, copyright 1989 by the Division of Christian Education of the National Council of the Churches of Christ in the USA. Used by permission. All rights reserved.

Scripture marked PHILLIPS is reprinted with the permission of the Macmillan Publishing Company from *The New Testament in Modern English* (PHILLIPS), Revised Student Edition, by J. B. Phillips, translator. Copyright 1958, 1960, 1972 by J. B. Phillips.

Scripture marked RSV is from the *Revised Standard Version* (RSV) of the Bible, copyright 1946, 1952, 1971 by the Division of Christian Education of the National Council of the Churches of Christ in the USA. Used by permission.

Scripture marked TLB is from *The Living Bible* (TLB), © 1971. Used by permission of Tyndale House Publishers, Inc., Wheaton, IL 60189. All rights reserved.

10   9   8   7   6   5   4   3   2   1

Contents

Foreword

I HAVE AT LEAST THREE THINGS IN COMMON with David McKenna. One, he is my predecessor as president of Asbury Theological Seminary. Two, we are both "converts" to Methodism. We came from different Christian backgrounds and were converted in other denominations. So, we both deliberately chose the Wesleyan way. That may be the reason for our third thing in common: a passion for Wesleyan distinctives.

As you read this book you will see that David McKenna is Evangelical about the Wesleyan distinctives of the Christian faith. I share that same enthusiastic commitment. I believe that we in the Wesleyan Methodist branches of the Christian Church have a unique contribution to make to the Church Universal, and we need to be Evangelical in offering that to the world. Without apology Dr. McKenna makes the claim that scriptural holiness, defined in biblical and Wesleyan terms, is a Spirit-guided corrective for our theological confusion, political contradistinction, and personal chaos. So he has served us well in writing this book, giving us convincing reasons why it is a great time to be a Wesleyan. Here in this volume is the essence of the Wesleyan way.

The reader will discover that Dr. McKenna is a masterful communicator. He breaks down what could be complex truth claims into easily accessible expressions of experience. For instance, he talks about sanctifying grace as a growing, hallowing, giving grace. Then, in an entire chapter on sanctification, he gives meaning to this issue that is too often debated but not often enough experienced. He defines sanctification as one holy passion, that is, our faithfulness to the will of God.

He uses classic and contemporary resources: Augustine and Samuel Rutherford along with Charles Colson and Billy Graham. He calls on theological perspectives as diverse as Harvey Cox and John Stott. He uses the disciplines of science, psychology, history, sociology, and social commentary to ground his message in contemporary life.

The book is shot through with personal testimony, which gives an experiential authenticity that is too often missing from theological writing. He is confessional in his sharing, opening the windows to his own soul, thus giving us a glimpse of an exciting pilgrimage on which he has deliberately walked for over 40 years. While this book offers a convincing apologetic for the Wesleyan distinctives of the Christian life, it gives a challenging description of the practical way the Wesleyan understanding of the gospel and Christian life is lived out.

One primary expression is that of personal and social holiness. Personal holiness—our response to the gospel giving us hearts of compassion, which welcomes strangers to our communities of faith and reaches out to the poor. Social holiness, which gives us a quickened conscience to all the issues that impact our daily lives and the corporate communities of which we are a part.

The sweep of salvation history is here. Prevenient grace—that wooing love of God that reaches out to us even when we are unaware. Justifying grace—that unmerited love of God that is universally offered and that accepts us where we are but does not leave us as we are; grace that, when we accept it by faith, makes us right with God. Sanctifying grace—that grace that continues to work in our lives, restoring the image of God within us and growing us up into the likeness of Christ.

The reader who is already a Wesleyan will celebrate that which he or she has already claimed and will find here the resources to share that heritage in a more convincing and contagious way. The reader who does not know the Wesleyan way will find here a clear presentation of a distinctive understanding of the gospel and Christian life that has contributed immensely to the Kingdom enterprise since the revival started after John Wesley's heartwarming experience at Aldersgate on May 24, 1738. What a time to be a Wesleyan!

—Maxie D. Dunnam, President
Asbury Theological Seminary

Meg's Memos

Dear Herbert,

Here's a bit of information that you won't find in this book!! My family and I lived in Spring Arbor from 1925-1930, then we moved from Michigan to Tucson. I still write to several friends that still life there, and that I went to school with. It is a wonderful school and town, and has one of the largest and most beautiful churches I have ever seen. The bell that had been in the tower, and that we 'kids' rang, is still there. We went back there for a reunion in 1982 and saw so many that we knew. This year they are celebrating 125 years. We met the current President, James Chapman, at a reunion in Phoenix two years ago.

Information manager,

Meg ︿︿
‿

Preface

I AM A WESLEYAN BY CHOICE. As a college freshman at Spring Arbor College in the late 1940s, I heard for the first time Charles Wesley's monumental words, "O for a thousand tongues to sing my great Redeemer's praise." The power of the song gripped my soul and brought from its depths a wellspring of praise that I had never known before. Already a Christian, I chose to be a Wesleyan and joined the Free Methodist Church.

A career in Christian higher education spanning 45 years took me from professor to president in a Wesleyan college, university, and seminary. Along the way, I moved easily across the lines of sister denominations for fellowship and ministry with Nazarenes, Wesleyans, Christian and Missionary Alliance, Salvation Army, Church of God (Anderson), and others. As president of Asbury Theological Seminary, a freestanding Wesleyan seminary, I developed warm working relationships with the United Methodist Church and its leaders, even when my heart bled with those who saw the church drifting from its moorings. The seminary presidency also opened wide the doors for me to sit and speak on behalf of our Wesleyan and Holiness heritage in the highest chambers of the World Methodist Council. In a small and personal way, the Wesleyan world is my parish.

I write this book in gratitude to my Wesleyan friends worldwide. May the words express my appreciation for the movement that adopted me, nurtured me, and gave me all of the opportunities of a natural son. Also, I want to communicate the strength of our identity as a people who believe, experience, and practice scriptural holiness in both its personal and social dimensions. Most of all, my goal is to lean outward toward the future and see Wesleyans as a people saved to serve in the turbulent times of the 21st century. Against the inevitable despair of a secular world and the dark pessimism of some theological traditions, Wesleyans are called to sing of grace and see God at work in human redemption until He himself declares the end.

Special thanks go to Neil Wiseman, an editor for Beacon Hill Press of Kansas City, for urging me to write this book; to Grace Yoder, assistant to the archivist at Asbury Theological Seminary, for scouring the McKenna papers and sending me sources; to Bonnie Perry, author and product development editor at Beacon Hill Press of Kansas City, for putting a refining, sensitive touch on the manuscript; and to Janet, my wife, who has so graciously accepted the fact that her husband retired from the ministry of administration to open a new chapter in the ministry of writing.

With His joy,
David L. McKenna

1 ═ Timely Heritage

"Wesleyans are a people saved to serve in turbulent times."

IMAGINE YOURSELF AS A CHILD peering into a kaleidoscope. Thousands of tiny, multicolored pieces form a dazzling mosaic before your eyes. With just the slightest turn of the eyepiece, all of the pieces tumble into a new and equally intriguing pattern. Now, set the eyepiece spinning again. Your vision blurs before the ever-tumbling, clashing pieces. Your mind cannot move fast enough to see a pattern in the chaos.

The spinning kaleidoscope characterizes our world today. The luxury of a stable society is gone forever. Change is constant and leaves us intellectually frustrated, emotionally exhausted, and spiritually challenged. The future bodes no better. We seem destined to learn to live with *speeding change, increasing complexity, and growing contradictions*. We stand on the edge of a society spinning out of control.

AN UPSIDE-DOWN WORLD

John Wesley would feel right at home in our turbulent times. Although 200 years have passed since Wesley lived and ministered in the late 18th century, he, too, faced the challenge of a society that seemed to be spinning out of control. Historians tell us 18th-century England was a crumbling culture. The corruption at its core included broken homes, child abuse, alcohol addiction, lewd theater, disenfranchised minorities, and impoverished lower classes. These were

11

symptoms of a society in which government was corrupt, law was biased, churches were irrelevant, and commerce was greedy. Only a miracle could save John Wesley's England from a bloody revolution.

We, too, are living with the reality of a crumbling culture that is corrupt at the core. The symptoms of moral breakdown and institutional paralysis that characterized 18th-century England are almost identical to the issues that trouble us today. Our leadership has lost credibility. Primary institutions like home, church, and school have broken down. Moral consensus has become a confused and contradictory shambles. Wherever we search for solutions—whether in politics, law, education, economics, or religion—we come up empty-handed. Are we at the point where only a miracle can save our civilization from bloody revolution or moral meltdown?

DYING AND DAWNING AGES

What in the world is happening? Again, we return to the time of John Wesley when 18th-century England was going through the throes of transition between the age of agriculture and the age of industry. Historians call this transition between two ages a "time of parenthesis." Kipling gives this idea its emotional context in his poetry when he sees the dying of one age and the dawning of another age as a time in which "one is dead; the other is helpless to be born."

From the Death of Agriculture to the Dawn of Industry. In Wesley's time, the dying age of agriculture centered on a farm economy with the *land* as wealth, *human labor* as capital, and the *accumulation of land* as the point of power. Enter the invention of the steam engine. The stable and slow-moving culture of the age of agriculture was upset forever. As the steam engine brought on the age of industry, all of the traditional resources of wealth, capital, and power broke down. Land gave way to *money* as the source of wealth, human labor gave way to *machines* as the source of capital, and the accumulation of land gave way to the *accumulation of money* as the point of power.

John Wesley lived in the time between the dying age of agriculture and the dawning age of industry. No transition in human history is more difficult than the time between ages, and human beings are dragged into the future kicking and screaming. Consider the 18th-century farmer in England who saw his first steam engine huffing and puffing along a railroad track. He took one look and said, "There has to be a horse in there someplace!"

The social impact of the dawning age of industry was not so humorous. Families on the move from the farm to the factory could no longer be the source of nurture they once were. Stodgy churches, connected to the crown, failed to move with the people and respond to their needs. Elitist schools, symbols of a rigid class system, catered only to the privileged. England almost lost its soul as a result. Although the change between the age of agriculture and the age of industry may have been slower and less complex than the change we face today, the chaos and contradictions had the same rending effect upon individual behavior and the social order.

From the Death of Industry to the Dawn of Information. The invention of the computer in the 20th century parallels the invention of the steam engine in the 18th century. Whether or not we recognize it, we are living in the time of transition between the dying age of industry and the dawning age of information. As surely as money replaced land as the source of wealth in Wesley's time, *information* has replaced money as the source of wealth in our time. Not only that, but *electronic circuits* have replaced traditional machines as the source of capital and the *control of information* has replaced the accumulation of money as the source of power. As the technology improved and information exchange became possible at unthinkable speeds, the social order has trembled on the edge of change. Like the spinning kaleidoscope, increasing speed brings on complexity and an invitation to chaos.

All is not lost. Students of society see the time of transition from the age of industry to the age of information as another "time of parenthesis." Think of the age of industry as past history; think of the age of information as future history. Between the two ages, then, insert "a time of parenthesis" with all of the chaotic conditions of cataclysmic social change. We have no choice. This is the turbulent time in which we are called to be Christians of Wesleyan conviction. Change is our challenge, speed is our nemesis, complexity is our dilemma, and chaos is our reality.

Our Wesleyan Challenge

How did John Wesley respond to the challenge of his time? He could have played it safe. As Peter Block writes in his book *Stewardship,* a person who wants to play it safe can become a *cynic* who criticizes society, a *victim* who blames others for the problems, or a *bystander* who refuses to get involved. None of these responses is worthy of a servant of Jesus Christ. None is worthy of the name Wesleyan. *Under the mandate and motivation of the Holy Spirit, John Wesley saw in the chaos of his time the challenge of spiritual regeneration for individuals and moral transformation for society.*

Because he had the vision and took the risk, England experienced a spiritual awakening that saved the nation from bloody revolution.

A GENIUS FOR SIMPLE TRUTH

To communicate his vision to ordinary people, John Wesley exercised his genius for putting a whole truth into a simple sentence. He summed up his theology in the four words "faith working through love." He spoke his vision in the phrase "the world is my parish." He packed a full theory of economics into the triplet "make all you can, save all you can, give all you can." He put controversy among Christians into perspective, "In essentials, unity; in non-essentials, liberty: in all things, charity." Perhaps best of all is the discovery that the stern and methodical Oxford don had a sense of humor. When told that his contentious wife had left him, some asked Wesley what effect it would have upon his ministry. He put the matter to rest: "I did not leave her; I did not ask her to leave; I will not ask her back." Finally, in a day when we are struggling with differences even within our Evangelical faith, we could well give heed to Wesley's irenic spirit when he wrote in *The Character of a Methodist,* "Do you love God and serve others? It is enough, give me your hand."

Make no mistake. John Wesley did not come to simple truth for the masses by short-circuiting the theological complexities and moral contradictions of his age. As Oliver Wendell Holmes said, "I would not give a fig for the simplicity this side of complexity; but I would give anything for the simplicity beyond complexity." Wesley had that genius. In his preaching, writing, and public conversation he communicated biblical truth with the simplicity beyond complexity.

Critics who have declared that Wesley was weak in his theology are wrong. Although he had the understanding to write a systematic theology for scholars, he chose to speak with a practical theology for the people. In the quiet of his reflective moments, in conversation with his colleagues, and in communion with the Holy Spirit he worked through the contradictions that confound us.

All eternal truth comes in the form of a paradox—facts that appear to contradict but are equally true. We cannot speak about the virtues of truth, goodness, and beauty without acknowledging the opposites of falsehood, evil, and ugliness. Likewise, theology begins with the paradoxical truth about God and Satan, sin and righteousness, justice and mercy, heaven and hell.

Most of us are uncomfortable in the presence of paradox. We struggle with the contradictions and tend to overemphasize one side or the other. On the job, we find it hard to be an independent individual and a team player at the same time. In the home, we waffle between our parental responsibilities for loving and disciplining our children at the same time. In the church, we struggle with the tension of responding to Jesus' call for us to be, at one and the same time, a leader and a servant.

Creative minds welcome paradox. Niels Bohr, the Nobel prizewinning scientist, said, "When we confront paradox, we know that we are on to something." In the same vein theologian Kierkegaard wrote, "The paradox is the source of the thinker's passion, and the thinker without paradox is like a lover without feeling; a paltry mediocrity." How did Wesley deal with paradox?

First, Wesley welcomed paradox in shaping his theology. To distinguish his Arminian position from the Calvinists, Wesley had to deal with the paradox of divine sovereignty and human freedom. He also had to struggle with the paradox of eternal security and falling from grace. We cannot consider the four points of the Wesleyan quadrilateral (reason, revelation, tradition, experience) that summarize our theology without remembering that they are couched in apparent paradox. The tension is apparent: reason *versus* revelation and tradition *versus* experience. As with Niels Bohr, Wesley sensed that when he confronted the contradictions, he knew that he was on to something.

Second, Wesley sought the mind of the Holy Spirit in working through the paradox of truth. The options for dealing with paradox are limited. We can either succumb to the tension of trying to hold two seemingly contradictory truths together, choose to emphasize one side to the neglect of the other, or seek to understand the higher truth that holds the two truths together in delicate balance. Here is where the Holy Spirit becomes our Teacher.

Wesleyan theology puts a premium upon the work of the Holy Spirit in our thinking as well as in our feeling and doing. When we are confronted with paradox, the mind of the Holy Spirit serves as the gyroscope that keeps us on balance against opposing forces and in speeding times. Through the mind of the Holy Spirit, Wesley resolved the paradox of divine sovereignty versus human freedom. He embraced the higher truth of prevenient grace, which nudges us toward Christ even before we are redeemed. Concerning the paradox of eternal security versus falling from grace, the Holy Spirit led Wesley to the oft-neglected doctrine of assurance by which His Spirit witnesses with our spirit that we are children of God.

Wesleyan theology is a delicate balance of paradoxical truth held together by the mind of the Holy Spirit. The beauty of this relationship is that the either-or of two opposite truths become the both-and of a higher truth. Elton Trueblood once labeled the little word *and* as the "holy conjunction." Wesleyans will be quick to agree. Inspired by the Holy Spirit, for instance, we do not speak of the nature of Jesus Christ as God *versus* man, but as the One who is fully God *and* fully man. In the power of the holy conjunction, we see the beauty of our faith.

Third, John Wesley led the masses with the simple truth beyond the complexity found in paradox. In his provocative book titled *Leading Minds: An Anatomy of Paradox,* Howard Gardner writes short biographies about persons whom he considers "leading minds" of the 20th century. Examples include Mahatma Gandhi, Martin Luther King, Margaret Mead, Eleanor Roosevelt, and Pope John XXIII. Gardner noted the common stroke of genius that each of them had for communicating with simplicity to the masses after struggling privately with the complexity of intellectual, social, and moral dilemmas. When they spoke to their professional colleagues, they talked of complexity, but when addressing their followers, their message was so simple that even a five-year-old child could understand.

Although John Wesley precedes by two centuries the contemporary leaders chosen by Gardner in his study, he led by the same principles. Wesley welcomed the challenge of chaotic times, struggled with the complexity of paradox, and led his followers with a word of hope that even a child could understand.

A TRIAD OF TRUTH

What would John Wesley say to us today? In 1982, as I prepared for my presidency at Asbury Theological Seminary, I took a sabbatical as a visiting scholar at Wesley Theological College, Cambridge University. My purpose was to read the primary sources of Wesley's journal, sermons, and letters in order to discover the genius of his leadership. Not by surprise, I found that Wesley exemplified all of the qualities of a visionary leader. He communicated a redemptive vision with simplicity that engaged the imagination of ordinary people; he personified that vision in every phase of his life and ministry; he created an organization that brought the vision to reality; and he held himself and his followers accountable to God and each other achieving the redemptive results. I came home with three simple sentences that I believe represent the genius of Wesley for living and witnessing as Wesleyans in a spinning world of chaos. If you listen, you can hear Wesley speaking to us now.

If You Can't Think It, Don't Believe It

Wesley's first word comes to us in the simple truth, *"If you can't think it, don't believe it."* Most of us have struggled with the paradox between divine revelation and human reason. Our tendency is to overemphasize one or the other. We have seen this conflict drive a wedge between Christians over the inspiration and authority of Scripture. Some have gone so far as to narrow down the meaning of Scripture to proof texts in verses and to theological positions in single words. At the other extreme are those in the camp of higher criticism who have used human reason to strip the Scriptures of their divine origin. Although this conflict rises and falls within the Christian community from time to time, the paradox remains. According to polls, many Evangelical Christians hold strongly to the belief in divine revelation but interpret the Word according to their own liking. Still others try to escape the tough questions of paradoxical truth by embracing a "generic evangelical faith" that dilutes biblical truth in favor of "seeker sensitivity" and social acceptance.

Wesley did not shy away from the complex questions regarding divine revelation and human reason. Without reservation, he declared his conviction about the inspiration and authority of Scripture when he said, "I am a man of one book." Yet, what he believed was never separated from what he thought. To the end of his life, Wesley remained the tough-minded but tenderhearted Oxford don. He read the classics while on horseback and relished what he called the "honest art" of intellectual debate. Behind the tight logic of his sermons is his premise that the way to the heart is through the head. In fact, a study of his converts shows they were "convinced" of the faith before they were "converted" to the faith. Wesley would be the first to agree with Elton Trueblood, the 20th-century Christian statesman who said, "The vocation of Christians in every generation is to outthink all the opposition." He would also agree with Charles Malik, the great Christian statesman from Lebanon, who said in his inaugural address for the opening of the Billy Graham Center, "Our mission is twofold. We must save souls and we must save minds." No wonder that Henry Rack titled his book on Wesley as *The Reasonable Enthusiast.* John Wesley left all Wesleyans the legacy that, under the guidance of the Holy Spirit, divine revelation and human reason are companions in the search and discovery of truth.

A Balloon, a Birdcage, and a Kite. Kierkegaard, the Danish theologian, warns against detached heads and detached hearts in his book *Purity of Heart Is to Will One Thing.* The head, he says, is the source of critical thinking, and the heart is the center for conscious convictions. A detached head knows no absolutes and advances no convictions. The result is a *secular subjectivism* in which pluralistic gods fill an oblong blur. As we have seen the course of mainline denominations in our century, we know what Kierkegaard means. We've opened arms to Eastern religions, New Age cults, humanistic notions, and antibiblical preferences under the umbrella of "pluralism." John Stott likens the thinking of a detached head to a helium-filled balloon that is out of control because it has no tether.

A detached heart, on the other hand, embraces blind belief, exempt from the discipline of critical thinking. The result is *religious irrationalism*. As one parishioner put it, "Whenever I go to church, I feel like unscrewing my head and placing it under the seat because in religious meetings I never have use for anything above my collar button." Stott pictures this kind of thinking as a bird in a cage—there is no freedom and no escape.

Neither secular subjectivism nor religious irrationalism is worthy of the Wesleyan mind that acknowledges God as the source of all truth. Head and heart should cohere in the adventures of critical thinking and in the affirmations of settled convictions. John Stott's analogy for this kind of thinking is the kite that soars freely into the sky but never comes loose from its tether.

Our oldest son, Douglas, holds a doctorate in psychology and is general manager for human resources at Microsoft. As part of his voracious reading schedule, he cleaned out my Wesley library to find out for himself the meaning of his heritage. After reading Wesley's journal, biographies, and history, he sat down at his computer in the middle of the night and began to write his findings. Number one was the simple sentence, "Perfect love is a present possibility." In explanation, he said that he could never work through the complexity of the doctrine of sanctification in his earlier years, but after reading Wesley he had no doubt. Through the truth of divine revelation and the discipline of human reason, the Holy Spirit had shown him that sanctification centers in the motivation of the heart, not the method of achievement nor the perfection of behavior. Through the message and model of Wesley himself, he came to the conviction that "perfect love is a present possibility."

Our Wesleyan Prayer. Revelation and reason must be united in our Christian faith. There is no other way in which we can do battle for the minds and hearts of men and women in a spinning, chaotic world. Wesley would be the first to join with the apostle Paul in his scriptural declaration: "The weapons we fight with are not the weapons of the world. On the contrary, they have divine power to demolish strongholds. We demolish arguments and every pretension that sets itself up against the knowledge of God, and we take captive every thought to make it obedient to Christ" (2 Cor. 10:4-5).

Charles Wesley's 18th-century plea still stands as a keynote for 21st-century Wesleyans: "Let us unite these two, so long divided, learning and vital piety."

If You Can't Sing It, Don't Preach It!

In the echoes of John Wesley, I think he would say to us today, "If you can't sing it, don't preach it!" In these words, he would show us how he dealt with the paradox of grace and truth. Wesleyans are a people known for their emphasis upon the gift of grace—the unmerited favor of God. At the same time, Wesleyans are people of the Word of God—the unequivocal truth of God. How can this paradox be resolved?

John Wesley was the preacher of the Wesleyan revival. His brother Charles was the poet. The preacher and the poet—a paradox itself. We think of a preacher as the one who proclaims the truth and the poet as the one who sings of grace. Truth and grace—opposites that are equally true within themselves and yet, with the enlightenment of the Holy Spirit, become one in the revelation of higher truth. John and Charles Wesley found that higher truth in the principle that "faith working through love" had to be sung as well as preached. This is practical theology at its best. When the brothers Wesley climbed the steps of the market cross to sing and preach the gospel in such industrial cities as Bristol and Liverpool, they saw people in despair. A narrowed Puritan theology had led many to believe that they were hopelessly damned, and a false deistic philosophy convinced them that God did not care. Then, cutting through the gloom and rising above the curses, came the pure sound of Charles Wesley singing the hymn that he wrote to celebrate the first anniversary of his conversion to Christ:

> *O for a thousand tongues to sing*
> *My great Redeemer's praise,*
> *The glories of my God and King,*
> *The triumphs of His grace!*
>
> *Jesus! the name that charms our fears,*
> *That bids our sorrows cease;*
> *'Tis music in the sinner's ears,*
> *'Tis life, and health, and peace.*
>
> *He breaks the pow'r of cancelled sin;*
> *He sets the pris'ner free.*
> *His blood can make the foulest clean;*
> *His blood availed for me.*

He speaks, and list'ning to His voice,
New life the dead receive.
The mournful, broken hearts rejoice;
The humble poor believe.

With the message of this melody sung in the musical idiom of the day, the brawling masses came to rapt attention as John Wesley began to preach.

Of Ditties and Dogma. What we sing is not always what we preach. In the current contest between contemporary and traditional styles of worship, the paradox between grace and truth is revealed. There is the temptation to come down hard on one side or other. Great hymns are canceled by the platitudes of cheap grace, or powerful preaching is made ludicrous by ditties of easy faith. Only the awesome presence of the Holy Spirit can bring grace and truth together. There is nothing wrong with exalting God or His grace through singing, but neither the complexity of His holiness nor the cost of Christ's cross can be ignored.

A quick study of the Wesley hymns shows the genius of the brothers in resolving the paradox of grace and truth in the popular tunes of the day so that even the simplest could understand. How else can we explain the personalized touch of sound biblical theology when we hear the words, "His blood can make the foulest clean; / His blood availed for me"? The test of any spiritual song, traditional or contemporary, is to hear the song of God's grace sung within the confession of human sin and the cost of Christ's cross. Whether in song or sermon, grace without this truth is cheap grace indeed.

Ellsworth Kalas, in his book *Our One Song,* says that Methodists are known as "singing people," not because we are obligated to sing, but because we have something to sing about. Feeble songs are the first sign of lost truth. In Alan Paton's historical novel *Ah, but Your Land Is Beautiful,* he tells the story of the people of South Africa whose beauty of spirit confounds the demeaning violence of apartheid when that was the policy of the nation. But the price of truth is costly. In Paton's story, Wilberfore Nhlapo, principal of an African high school, chooses his pension and his position rather than stand for the cause of freedom with his people. When he does, fear sets in and he seeks the counsel of a friend, saying, "Robert, it's all gone. The happiness is gone, the fear has returned. The jolly laughing man is gone. I ask myself if he will ever come back again." His compromise with truth cost him his jolly, laughing spirit.

As Wesleyans, we must never compromise on biblical truth that costs us the joy of our singing. It is through the spirit of our songs and the strength of our preaching that others see the balance of grace and truth. Paul the apostle sang just such a song in Romans when he weighed sin in the balance against grace and then burst out singing, "Yet, though sin is shown to be wide and deep, thank God his grace is wider and deeper still!" (Rom. 5:20, PHILLIPS).

In an age of chaos and a time of paradox, the Word of truth accented by the note of grace still rings loud and clear above the brawling masses.

If You Can't Live It, Don't Push It!

Today, John Wesley might well say to us, "If you can't live it, don't push it!" With these words, he would be dealing with the paradox between "being" and "doing" that continues to hound us in our generation. Conservative Christians tend to be identified with the "born again" experience and its redeeming influence upon the "being" of the person. Not long ago, we had a larger image. Timothy Smith, noted American historian, reminds us in *Revivalism and Social Reform* that in the 19th century conservative Christians led the way as "doers" of the faith—with their leadership as opponents of slavery, advocates of labor reform, and champions of the poor, the sick, the orphaned, and the elderly. After the turn of the 20th century, however, conservative Christians retreated into a defense of "being" at the expense of "doing." Liberal Christians, then, picked up the leadership role and pushed "doing" to the extreme of the "social gospel." Today, though both camps have moved toward the other, the division remains. Conservative Christians are best known for a personal emphasis upon "being" while liberal Christians are identified with a social emphasis upon "doing."

John Wesley would be appalled to hear that contemporary Wesleyans have lost the "holy conjunction" of both being *and* doing. To Wesley, personal holiness meant the perfection of love for every conscious motive in the believer's life. At the same time, he saw the inseparable connection of this love with social holiness. In a pungent statement of simple truth, Wesley said, "The gospel of Christ knows of no religion, but social; no holiness, but social holiness." He backed up that conviction in his practice.

After nonbelievers were convinced by Wesley's preaching, they were invited to a class meeting where they could learn more about the gospel and also see if Methodists practiced the faith and love they professed. Once converted, then, even the poorest were expected to give a penny a week to those who were poorer still. As these new believers grew in grace, social holiness had two dimensions: increasing spiritual accountability to the Body of Christ and greater social responsibility for the needs of the poor. Maturing members of the Methodist class meeting were expected to reach out in ministries to prisoners, widows, the aged, the sick, the hungry, and especially to oppressed children.

Wesley would expect the same personal accountability and social responsibility of us today. Any division between personal and social holiness is unbiblical. John Wesley would be dismayed by the division. He would warn those who lock arms with violent protesters in a march for justice under the banner of social holiness. He would be equally firm with those who remain isolated from the problems of the poor in the name of personal holiness.

After my retirement as president of Asbury Theological Seminary, my first task was to update the history of my church under the title *A Future with a History: The Wesleyan Witness of the Free Methodist Church.* As part of my research, I reread the story of our founding in order to discover the core convictions that motivated and mobilized our people for a march across America during the second half of the 19th century. At the center of those convictions was the doctrine of entire sanctification, or personal holiness. But the doctrine did not stand alone. Personal holiness was inseparably connected with compassion for the poor that was evidenced, not just by free seats in the churches and advocacy of abolition in the culture, but by risky ventures of self-giving to unwed mothers, orphaned children, and homeless men. Suddenly, it dawned upon me. If either personal or social holiness is disconnected from the other, neither makes sense.

Therefore, when Holiness people forfeited the field of social holiness to liberals around the turn of the century, we lost the reason for the stewardship of holy living, which gave the movement its distinctive character. Our separation from the world makes sense only when there is engagement with the world through the ministry of self-giving to the poor, needy, and disenfranchised among us. With great regret, I concluded that we lost the vitality of the Holiness Movement and the meaning of the doctrine of entire sanctification because we disconnected personal holiness from social holiness in the ministry of compassion. Consequently, we have fallen victim to the sweep of the broad brush that identifies Evangelical Christians as social protesters with a selective agenda and political motive. This is a high price for the separation of personal holiness and social holiness.

WESLEY'S WORD OF WISDOM

John Wesley would reserve a special word for Evangelical Christians who are venturing back into the arena of political reform and social action today. Recalling his own experience from the 18th century, Wesley would remind us that he vigorously resisted public pressure to make him a leader in social reform as he gained national prominence on the high tide of spiritual revival. Not until the movement of Methodism proved it credible as a genuine spiritual force for personal redemption and social renewal in the culture did Wesley raise his voice to speak against slavery. But then, when he spoke, everyone listened.

Divisive issues engulf us—racism, abortion, poverty, sexism, hunger, violence, pollution, homosexuality, AIDS, abuse—the list could go on and on. Wesleyans must respond to these issues. We must demonstrate once again the meaning of "faith working through love." In our own lives first, we must establish the credibility for our social witness through the transforming power of our redemptive influence. In support of this witness, we must show evidence of self-giving compassion to the victims of these social ills. Then and only then can we address these issues at the level of justice as well as mercy. Economic justice, for instance, is no longer on the Evangelical agenda. I am convinced that if John Wesley were alive today, he would conclude that we affluent Wesleyans do not push for economic justice because we do not want to live it. Yet, if Walhburt in his book *The Coming Third Church* is right, our prayers for spiritual revival will not be heard until we become stewards of our wealth serving the poor at home and the impoverished abroad.

In the middle of the 1970s, the syndicated columnist James Reston asked, "What difference will the 'Born-again Movement' make in the moral pigsty of our secular culture?" Only the verdict of history can answer his question. As it stands now, our society seems to be more corrupt, more violent, and more secular than ever. If so, is it possible that conservative Christians are trying to reform society by political pressure, legislative action, and judicial ruling before our credibility as a redemptive influence has been clearly established among the masses? John Wesley would remind us of the inseparable link between personal and social holiness. Just as he made personal holiness the motive for social holiness, he made spiritual credibility the prerequisite for leadership in social reform. Regarding social holiness, he would agree with Elton Trueblood, who said, "One cannot give what one does not have." Conversely, with regard to personal holiness, Wesley would add, "One cannot have what one does not give."

WESLEY'S WORD FOR TODAY

Can you hear John Wesley speaking to us today? Although we know that no one can put a piece of carbon paper over the 18th century and apply it to the age in which we live, we also know that truth is timeless. Listen again. John Wesley has a word for us.

- *If You Can't Think It, Don't Believe It!*—a plea for uniting revelation and reason in our Wesleyan faith.
- *If You Can't Sing It, Don't Preach It!*—a plea for balancing truth and grace in our Wesleyan worship, and
- *If You Can't Live It, Don't Push It!*—a plea for connecting personal and social holiness in our Wesleyan witness.

There is no doubt. Wesleyans have the heritage of the biblical message revealed by the Holy Spirit as simple truth for ordinary people. Because this message is most readily heard in turbulent times, it is still true for today and tomorrow. With full confidence we can seize the moment and exclaim, *"Thank God, What a Time to Be a Wesleyan!"*

2

Gift of Grace

"Wesleyans are a people who know the joy of grace, freely received and freely given."

GRACE, THE FREE AND UNDESERVED GIFT OF GOD by which we are saved, is at the heart and soul of Wesleyan belief and experience. This is not as obvious as it may seem. Christian theology balances on a pinpoint between grace and truth. To maintain that balance is not easy. In some generations, the more gentle doctrine of grace prevails. In others, the relentless pursuit of truth takes over. Puritan preaching in Colonial America back in the 1700s, for instance, is remembered for its stern truth. Jonathan Edwards, a great preacher of that era, is best known for his sermon "Sinners in the Hands of an Angry God." As he preached, the hard truth of hell became so real to his listeners that they took a white-knuckled grip on the pews to keep from falling into the flames. Of course, Edwards also preached the grace of God, but in the hard-nosed Calvinist mind of the Puritans, it tended to lose its beauty as a free and universal gift.

On the other extreme, we are firsthand witnesses of cheap grace in our day. In place of Jonathan Edwards's hellfire and brimstone preaching of hard truth, we have the soft soap and sugary preaching of easy grace. A lasting memory comes to mind. In the setting of a world congress on evangelism, the keynote speaker preached from Acts 2:37 when those who heard Peter's sermon at Pentecost were "cut to the heart" and asked the disciples, "Brothers, what shall we do?" Another prominent preacher of media fame, hearing the words, got up and walked out of the meeting. After the meeting, he held a session in the lobby where he declared that modern people will not listen to the hard truth about conviction from sin anymore. Behind his protest lurked the suspicion that he viewed faith as easy and grace as cheap.

Wesleyans do not have a corner on grace. We do, however, have a responsibility to maintain the Spirit-guided balance between grace and truth. Our task is complicated by the fact that biblical grace is a paradox. At one and the same time, it is a gift that is costly and yet free. Its cost is written in the cross of Jesus Christ, and its free provision is written in God's "whosoever will." Wesleyans add another critical dimension to this paradox. We believe that grace is full as well as free. "Full," in this context, refers to the grace that is at work in every person, even before salvation, as the Holy Spirit uses an infinite variety of means to lead us to God. Furthermore, it is the fullness of grace that makes our sanctification possible. "Perfect love" and the "fullness of the Spirit" are synonymous terms.

Jesus himself is our model for balancing the paradox. He is described as a person "full of grace and truth" (John 1:14). This is the defining characteristic of spiritual beauty in human personality. To stress either grace or truth is to lose the "fullness" that gives our witness its distinguishing quality. Here again, our Wesleyan emphasis upon the work of the Holy Spirit comes into view. Only with His discerning mind can we keep the balance.

The good news is that the biblical understanding of full and free grace is being revived today. Perhaps motivated by Bill Moyers's telecast on "Amazing Grace," the message of full and free grace has once again found a match with the needs of people. Best-sellers in the late 1990s—such as *What's So Amazing About Grace?* by Phillip Yancey, *The Grace Awakening* by Charles Swindoll, *In the Grip of Grace* by Max Lucado, and *A Dangerous Hope* by Al Truesdale and Bonnie Perry—give testimony to this need and interest.

Wesleyans are remiss if we do not contribute to the discussion. In fact, we should be taking the lead with our emphasis upon the Holy Spirit as the agent of full and free grace. Otherwise, the balance can tip again toward an extreme of grace that is neither full nor free.

John Wesley himself shows us the fullness of grace in his own spiritual journey. In his early life history, we see the gift of grace shaping him for one of the most effective and far-reaching ministries in human history—leading him to God, saving him in Christ, and sanctifying him through the Holy Spirit. Wesley would be the first to reject the notion that we should be carbon copies of him, but with his confidence in God's grace, he would not hesitate to recommend that we accept the gift, full and free.

I. Leading Grace

John Wesley's spiritual journey begins with his birth in a Christian home where he learned obedience to the will of his parents and the will of God. Susanna, his strong-minded mother, set aside time every Thursday to talk with her son John, or "Jacky" as he was known, about obedience to the ways of righteousness. The young lad became so disciplined that his father, Samuel, told Susanna, "I do profess, sweetheart, I think that our Jack would not attend to the most pressing necessities of nature unless he could give a reason for it."

Wesley not only had the advantage of a Christian home but also had the privilege of a Christian school at Charterhouse. As a prodigious nine-year-old, he became the favorite of the faculty because his greatest sin was a game of cards and an occasional lapse in his "outward duties." Later, at Oxford, where he excelled in scholarship, his search for inward holiness turned to good work as leader of the Holy Club and still later to ordination as an Anglican priest. During that time, Wesley describes his preaching, "I drew no crowds; I alarmed no consciences; I influenced no lives; I preached much but saw no fruit for my labor."

The answer seemed to be the mission field. Sailing to Georgia, the land of exile for English debtors and criminals, Wesley took on the trappings of a high Anglican churchman. He donned all of the pieces of canonical garb and demanded such ritualistic perfection that the people of Georgia mistook him for a Roman Catholic priest. When he fled the colony under the threat of trial for allegedly alienating a young woman's affection, Wesley confessed, "I went to America to convert the Indians, but oh! who will convert me?"

Deep conviction followed Wesley from Georgia as a result of his shipboard encounter with a Moravian pastor named Spangenberg who dared to ask him, "Does the Spirit of God bear witness with your spirit that you are a child of God?" Wesley could not answer with assurance.

Once back in England, another Moravian named Peter Böhler had frequent walks with Wesley and "besought him to go to the open fountain, and not to mar the efficacy of free grace by his unbelief." Convicting grace settled over Wesley, so much so that he vowed never to preach again. Böhler, however, told him, "Preach faith 'til you have it, then because you have it, you will preach faith." Obeying his mentor, Wesley preached faith even to a prisoner named Clifford who was under the death sentence. Clifford just before his execution, then, testified to the faith that John Wesley preached, but did not know for himself, when he left this witness, "I am now ready to die. I know Christ has taken away my sins and there is no more condemnation."

Wesley reminds me of my friend Jack Eckerd, whose life story is told in the book *Eckerd: The Right Prescription.* Through a common interest in prison reform in Florida, Jack met Chuck Colson. Together they stumped the state on behalf of legislation for prison reform. At each stop, Jack Eckerd, a household name in Florida, introduced Colson the same way. "Hello, I'm Jack Eckerd. I'm here to introduce Chuck Colson to you. He's a born-again Christian and I'm not, but I wish I were." With such honesty, it is no surprise to learn that Jack soon became a believer himself.

Wesley was equally honest. He saw, through the teaching of Peter Böhler, that we are saved by faith alone, but he could still not accept the fact that the gift of grace could be freely given in a moment of time. When Böhler brought four witnesses who could testify to an instantaneous experience, Wesley demanded eight. All of the years of critical thinking and disciplined reasoning stood as the last barrier to his faith. Emotionally, however, the feelings of conviction gripped him as he wept while singing hymns of faith and prayed so earnestly, "The faith I want is a sure trust and confidence in God, that, through the merits of Christ, my sins are forgiven, and I am reconciled to the favor of God."

No wonder that as he left his house on the morning of Aldersgate, he opened his Bible once again and his eyes fell upon the words, "Thou art not far from the kingdom of God" (Mark 12:34, KJV). No wonder that at a quarter to nine, in an instant of time, Wesley felt his heart strangely warmed as he trusted in Christ and Christ alone. He could now testify with assurance that his sins, even his sins, were taken away.

Leading Grace at Work

In the life history of John Wesley leading up to Aldersgate, we see the dimensions of prevenient or "leading" grace at work. Prevenient grace is defined as the grace that "goes before us." It is *preventing grace* that kept John Wesley from gross sin; *awakening grace* that stirred in him the thirst for inward holiness; *surprising grace* by which God revealed himself through unexpected events. C. S. Lewis recounted how God kept surprising him when he was resisting the faith. "God is very unscrupulous," he wrote. "He makes sure that open Bibles are lying on tables wherever I go." Prevenient grace is also convicting grace that made Wesley weep because of unbelief. It is the leading grace that brought him to faith in Christ and Christ alone.

Prevenient grace is the Wesleyan answer to the Calvinist doctrine of predestination. Without diluting the nature of human sin or the sovereignty of God's will, we believe with Wesley that grace is "free in all, and free for all." Or as Bishop William Cannon envisions grace, "It is like the air we breathe or the wind that blows in our faces." God's prevenient grace goes before us—preventing us from sin, awakening in us a thirst for God, surprising us with His providence, convicting us of unbelief, and leading us to trust in Christ and Christ alone.

Leading Grace for Us

We need to rediscover the meaning of prevenient grace in our own lives as well as in the lives of people we are called to serve. The heavy weight of Freudian psychology has given us a negative fixation on our past. As I review best-selling Evangelical books, the past is almost always a "negative experience" we must overcome in order to achieve personal fulfillment. My E-mail filled up, for instance, during the presidential crisis in 1998. With an instant diagnosis, Christian counselors identified President Clinton's sexual problems as an addiction based upon an abusive childhood and an alcoholic father. By inference, if not by fact, his behavior is excused and responsibility is shifted to other people.

Prevenient grace gives us a different picture of our past. Some years ago I reviewed two magnificent books that are now part of my permanent library. One is titled *To Will God's Will* by Ben Campbell Johnson; the other is *Cry Pain, Cry Hope* by Elizabeth O'Connor. In each case, they recommend that we return to the practice of 18th-century Methodists and keep a journal of our spiritual walk. To begin, the suggestion is that we go back to the earliest memories of our lives and note the "marker events" that help us define who we are and how we got where we are today. Chapters in our journal are proposed for ages 1 to 6, from 6 to 12, 12 to 20, 20 to 40, 40 to 55, 55 to 70, and 70 until we are no longer able. The authors suggest that we name each chapter and then ask the question, "How was the Spirit of God at work in my life during this time?" Such a promising question is a radical departure from a downcast, self-excusing attitude toward our life history.

In my own case, I could fix upon being a child conceived out of wedlock and raised in a loveless, eventually broken home and rigid Holiness church. But as I reviewed the chapters of my life with the question in mind, "How was the Spirit of God at work in my life?" the whole perspective changed. Chapter 1 is titled "A Brand from the Burning" because my grandmother prayed all night for my healing when I was just six months old. The doctor had discovered a blood clot headed for my heart and declared it a life-or-death issue in the next 24 hours. During that night of prayer, the clot went across my back, down my arm and dissolved in the hand. Each succeeding chapter has its own title and witness of prevenient grace—sometimes preventing me from sin, at other times convicting me of sin, and always leading me toward faith in Jesus Christ.

Only two or three people know it, but I once wrote a novel of my life's story through childhood and adolescence until I enrolled in college. When I finished the book I chose the title *Amusing Grace* because looking back, so many marker events in my spiritual journey that might have turned me from God actually led me toward Him. How else can you account for the picture in the high school yearbook that shows the captain of the tennis team in long, white pants while all of the other members are in typical tennis shorts? I had been discovered wearing shorts during a practice match by a girl in the church who reported it to the pastor. Next Sunday's sermon centered on dress for Christians, including the prohibition against exposure in tennis shorts. I might have become bitter, but when I discovered the meaning of prevenient grace, I learned to laugh. Only grace can account for my salvation. Dare I say that the title of my unpublished novel, *Amusing Grace,* summarizes the spiritual journey for most of us?

On the Way to Aldersgate

Because of leading grace John Wesley's walk to Aldersgate does not begin at 8:45 P.M. on the evening on May 24, 1738. It starts on his spiritual journey as a child, youth, and young adult struggling through good works of righteousness, rationalism, formalism, and even mysticism. Although none of that could save him, each of these experiences was nudging him forward to the moment when he trusted in Christ, and Christ alone, for his salvation.

C. S. Lewis, in his sermon "The Weight of Glory," says that he has never met an ordinary person. He meant that he saw the gift of grace at work in every person he met. What an insight! To see the gift of prevenient grace at work in our own lives first, then in the lives of others, will transform our outlook and kindle our compassion. If we look, we will see evidence of the Spirit of God nudging every human being toward the saving grace of Christ.

Prevenient grace takes the mystery out of what God is doing in our lives. It also changes our view of people, institutions, movements, and cultures in the world. God is no arbitrary ruler, capricious gambler, or absentee landlord as far as our eternal destiny is concerned. In every person and in every movement, He is leading, convicting, pursuing, and drawing us toward His saving grace. God uses every means at His disposal to get our attention and lead us to faith. So, our spiritual journey may seem torturous and long, but make no mistake. God's will for us is good, and His goal for us is our salvation. On the road to Aldersgate with John Wesley, we see ourselves being led, convicted, pursued, and drawn by God's gracious Spirit until our thirst for righteousness brings us to the entrance of that narrow, little opening called Aldersgate Street.

II. SAVING GRACE

Aldersgate Day—May 24, 1738—is a drama in itself. Wesley awakened long before dawn to meditate, pray, and read the Bible. In his meditation, the panorama of his life from the age of 10 passed before his eyes. About 5 A.M. he opened the Word of God to read, "Whereby are given unto us exceeding great and precious promises: that by these ye might be partakers of the divine nature" (2 Pet. 1:4, KJV).

Then, just before he went out to the duties of the day, Wesley opened the Testament one more time to read, "Thou art not far from the kingdom of God." Aldersgate is a "marker point" along the road of John Wesley's spiritual journey. At the age of 35, this Oxford don, Lincoln Fellow, and Anglican priest went "very unwillingly" to a place on narrow Aldersgate Street in the north of London where someone was reading from Luther's *Preface to the Epistle to the Hebrews*. Wesley heard these pointed and personalized words:

Faith is the divine work in us, which changes us and makes us newly born of God, and kills the old Adam, makes us completely different men in heart, disposition, mind and every power, and brings the Holy Spirit with it. O faith is a lively, creative, active, powerful thing, so that it is impossible that it should not continually do good works. It does not even ask if good works are to be done, but before anyone asks, it has done them, and it is always acting.

Into the readiness of Wesley's heart, saving grace broke through to prompt this testimony, "I felt my heart strangely warmed; I felt I did trust in Christ, Christ alone, for salvation, and an assurance was given me that He had taken away my sins, even mine, and saved me from the law of sin and death."

Critics have tried to debunk or discount the Aldersgate experience. Some sweep it away as a "gust of feeling" or an "attack of indigestion." Others explain it naturally as the emotional rebound from a frustrated love affair with Sophia Hopkey. Still others put Wesley on the psychiatrist's couch and analyze his case as a classic example of a "sick soul" according to William James's book *Varieties of Religious Experience*. Some specifically note that Wesley mentions the experience only once in the next 50 years of journal writing. And for the sophisticated religionists of the staid Church of England, Aldersgate is ridiculed as "enthusiasm"—a pejorative term of which warmhearted Wesleyans have always been accused.

But Aldersgate is more than a "gust of feeling." In it we see the gift of God's saving grace with which any believer identifies. Wesley's own testimony reminds us that saving grace, through the work of the Holy Spirit, *regenerates* us in the image of Christ, *justifies* us in the Cross of Christ, and *assures* us of our salvation in the love of Christ.

The Feeling of Regeneration

Saving grace regenerates us in the image of Christ. Regeneration is the work of God through His Holy Spirit by which we are made new creatures in the image of Christ. Without doubt, Aldersgate was an emotional experience. Wesley, we remember, was a boy who wouldn't even attend to the necessities of life unless he had a reason; Wesley was the youth who rigidly controlled his behavior in the search for holiness; Wesley was the man who demanded ritual precision of his parishioners. Only a surprise to suppressed emotions could bring Wesley to burst forth with uncharacteristic joy, "I felt my heart strangely warmed." For the first time, he could admit feeling as well as fact, heart as well as head, surprise as well as order, and warmth as well as cold. Our spiritual experience is never complete without the "burst of feeling," the "surprise of miracle," and the "warmth of love."

I identify with Wesley. As a 12-year-old boy, I had built a wall of protective righteousness around my soul to hide the sin of my heart. One evening in the young people's service, my aunt devised a scheme of entrapment by asking that everyone give their testimony according to alphabetical order. Like the guy eating alphabet soup, I kept seeing my name come up. The countdown began, "A," "B," "C." When my aunt got down to "M" my grandfather, grandmother, father, mother, and even my 7-year-old sister testified. Everyone turned and looked at me. Breaking out in a cold sweat, I stood and confessed that I did not have peace in my heart and asked them to pray for me. My father met me at the altar and together we prayed for my salvation. Afterward, as we drove home in an old 1938 gray Plymouth, my dad began to sing, "There's a new name written down in glory." For the first time, I could join in the refrain, "And it's mine. O yes, it's mine!"

No one can take away from me the validity of that emotional experience. I understand why John Wesley and a troop of friends left Aldersgate Street singing at the top of their voices on the way to Charles Wesley's house. When they got there, John simply told his brother, "I believe," and another song broke out. This time they sang together the hymn that Charles wrote to celebrate his own conversion a few days earlier:

> *Where shall my wondering soul begin?*
> *How shall I all to heav'n aspire?*
> *A slave redeemed from death and sin,*
> *A brand plucked from eternal fire,*
> *How shall I equal triumphs raise*
> *Or sing my great Deliv'rer's praise?*

Regenerating grace makes us whole persons as well as new creatures in the image of Christ. As John Wesley illustrates so well, the strange, heartwarming experience balances the disciplined mind and obedient will that he brought to Aldersgate. Wesley needed the warmth of love to be a whole person. Our need today is just the opposite. We need the disciplined mind and obedient will to balance out emotional experiences and spiritual subjectivity. Alan Bloom, in *The Closing of the American Mind,* contends that the loss of absolute moral values and the distrust of reason have created an open vacuum into which emotion flows. The persons who really care (as opposed to those who are lukewarm in their commitments) receive special attention and special privileges for their "intensity" and "commitment." In other words, Bloom says that fanaticism replaces reason when emotional intensity is mistaken for moral integrity. A fanatic, by definition, is a person who acts as God would act—if God had all the facts! Perhaps this is why Wesley refused to overemphasize Aldersgate. He knew that it was a balancing event, not a standalone experience.

Intimacy is another quality of regenerating grace. Not by accident, Wesley uses the words "me," "my," and "mine" to describe his experience. God was no longer a philosophical abstraction or a theological construct. He became a living presence in personal relationship with Wesley. This was not easy. John Wesley was one of the strongest advocates for the sacraments as a means of grace—the mediating and indirect influences through which we relate to God and Christ. Although both sacraments and experience are balanced in faith development, Wesley put primacy upon the immediate, intimate, and direct encounter with God by which His Spirit invades our being and dwells within us.

The Fact of Justification

Saving grace justifies us in the cross of Christ. John Wesley speaks this truth at Aldersgate when he testifies, "I felt I did trust in Christ, Christ alone, for my salvation." Once again, we realize what it meant for Wesley to make this confession. He was a man of exemplary character and good works in search for salvation. Now, for the first time, he puts character and works aside to trust in Christ, and Christ alone.

Again, we stand before a monumental truth that is being neglected today. Justification by faith takes us directly to the saving grace of Jesus Christ. John Stott, in his book *The Cross of Christ,* presents these helpful images for understanding the full meaning of our salvation:

Propitiation is the image of the shrine. Here is Christ's atoning sacrifice to appease the wrath of God which we deserve;

Redemption is the image of the marketplace. Here Christ buys us back and sets us free from the captivity of sin;

Justification is the image of the law court. Here Christ becomes our substitute and accepts the sentence of our guilt; and

Reconciliation is the image of the home. Here Christ restores broken relationships for those who are alienated from the Father.

For Wesley, Aldersgate meant a shift in the center of gravity for his soul. No longer will he rely upon the works of intellectualism, moralism, ritualism, or mysticism for his salvation. In fact, he confesses that these are only "refined ways of relying upon our own works." Instead, he testifies that he was changed at Aldersgate from a servant to a son, from a man of law to a man of grace. Before Aldersgate, the name of Christ was only a formality in the benediction of his sermons. After Aldersgate, Wesley writes that he speaks continually of Jesus Christ, "Laying Him as the only foundation of the whole building, making Him all in all, the first and the last." Neither a disciplined mind nor an obedient will can justify us before God. As Paul writes to the Galatians, "I do not set aside the grace of God, for if righteousness could be gained through the law, Christ died for nothing!" (2:21).

Wesley's confession, "I trusted Christ and Christ alone," is to acknowledge, "It is finished." There is nothing to pay and he cannot make a contribution. Yet, as John Stott says, "We resent the idea that we cannot earn—or at least contribute to our own salvation. So, we stumble, as Paul put it, over the stumbling block of the cross of Christ."

Our need is the perspective on justifying grace that Toplady gives us in the hymn "Rock of Ages":

> *Nothing in my hands I bring,*
> *Simply to Thy cross I cling.*
> *Naked, come to Thee for dress;*
> *Helpless, look to Thee for grace;*
> *Foul, I to the fountain fly;*
> *Wash me, Savior, or I die!*

The Faith of Assurance

Saving grace assures us of our salvation in the love of Christ. In his Aldersgate testimony, Wesley says, "I felt . . . an assurance was given to me that He had taken away my sin, even mine, and saved me from the law of sin and death." John Wesley is often accused of being weak in theology. Nothing could be farther from the truth. For ordinary people, theology is humorously defined as giving elaborate answers to questions that no one is asking. If this is so, Wesley *is* weak on theology. When it comes to the questions that people are asking, however, Wesley is a giant in his field. For example, each of us asks the question, "How can I be sure of my salvation?" When nothing in classical theology could define his Aldersgate experience, Wesley turned to the Scriptures for help. He discovered the meaning of Aldersgate in Rom. 8:16, "The Spirit itself beareth witness with our spirit, that we are the children of God" (KJV). Before Aldersgate, he could not answer "Yes" when asked if he had the witness of the Spirit that he was a child of God. After Aldersgate, he answered "Yes" with complete confidence.

If Wesleyan theology has a litmus test for faith, it is the "witness of the Spirit." In this truth is the Wesleyan doctrine of assurance that joins prevenient grace as unique contributions to biblical theology and our Christian faith.

Certainty of salvation is always a dilemma. Although I was brought up in a church whose theology was obliquely Wesleyan, I never heard the doctrine of assurance emphasized as a distinctive of our heritage. Perhaps this is why I struggled for years with the dread of displeasing God, losing my faith, and going to hell.

At first, I thought that Calvinists had a corner on certainty. Then, I learned that John Calvin himself wrote that the saint's greatest struggle was the lack of certainty about salvation. Even with irresistible grace and the perseverance of the saints, there was no certainty of salvation until death. Roman Catholics depend upon the church for their certainty; Lutherans depend upon faith; Reformers depend upon doctrine. For the people called Wesleyans, however, our certainty is found in an affirmative answer to the question, "Have you the witness of the Spirit that you are a child of God?" With our affirmation comes His assurance.

III. SANCTIFYING GRACE

Aldersgate is not a stopping point along the way of John Wesley's spiritual journey. In his own testimony after Aldersgate, he sets the stage for going on. After speaking those oft-quoted words about a "heart, strangely warmed," he continues:

> I began to pray with all might for those who had in a more especial manner despitefully used me and persecuted me. I then testified openly to all there what I now first felt in my heart. But it was not long before the enemy suggested, "This cannot be faith; for where is thy joy?" Then was I taught that peace and victory over sin are essential to faith in the Captain of our salvation; but that, as to the transports of joy that usually attend the beginning of it, especially in those who have mourned, God sometimes giveth, and sometimes withholdeth them, according to the counsels of His will.

On the way to Aldersgate with John Wesley, we marveled at the evidence of prevenient grace—the grace that prevents us from sin, convicts us of sin, and leads us toward God and Christ. At Aldersgate with Wesley, we stood amazed in the strange and warming presence of saving grace—the grace that regenerates us as new creatures, justifies us before God, and assures us of salvation through the witness of the Spirit. Now, we come to the third towering truth in the Wesleyan trilogy of grace—the experience of sanctifying grace.

God's grace is the common denominator in each of these experiences. In Wesley's day, the announcement that God's grace was "free in all, and free for all" had the sound of spiritual reveille. Calvinism restricted the grace of God, deism had depersonalized it, Lutheranism had objectified it, Moravianism had mystified it, and Anglicanism had forgotten it. The Wesleys, however, made the free gift of God's grace the keynote of sermon and song. As they preached, they sang of the multiplied riches of grace: "sovereign grace," "quickening grace," "glorious grace," "infinite grace," "plenteous grace," "redeeming grace," "the counsels of His grace," "the riches of His grace," and "the whispers of His grace."

Equally important to our understanding of grace is the work of the Holy Spirit. Whether dealing with prevenient grace, saving grace, or sanctifying grace in our spiritual journey, we cannot forget that it is the person of the Holy Spirit through whom grace flows. To isolate His work in any one of these three experiences is to sever the thread of grace that God uses to draw us to himself, save us from ourselves, and sanctify us for others. In that context, we can understand the spiritual dilemma that Wesley faced after Aldersgate.

Growing Grace

When we speak of sanctifying grace, we begin with the evidence of *growing grace.* No one contests the fact that the Holy Spirit is given to the believer at the time of justification. For Wesleyans, it is also the time when the dynamic process of entire sanctification begins. After Aldersgate Wesley felt the goad to grow when Satan whispered to him, "Where is thy joy?" Even though Wesley testifies to the assurance of peace and joins in singing a hymn of redemption, he lacks a sense of joy. At best, he can say that God in His counsel decides when and if He gives the "transports of joy" to those who believe.

Critics of Wesley can find plenty of evidence that he struggled after Aldersgate. The morning after the emotional high of that night, he went into deep depression. Later on, in a moment of doubt, he writes in his journal, "I am not a Christian." Theologically, he struggled to the point of breaking with George Whitefield over the doctrine of sanctification. Experientially, he could not reconcile his Aldersgate experience with the "all or none" mysticism of the Moravians. And each of us remembers his miserable failures with women and marriage.

Growing grace is always painful. In the Gospel of John we read, "And of his fulness have all we received, and grace for grace" (John 1:16, KJV). Earl Palmer, in his book *Laughter in Heaven,* suggests that the literal meaning of "grace for grace" is "grace against grace." In other words, we need grace for the contradictions in our lives. None of us is exempt from the fault lines that also appeared in Wesley after Aldersgate—moments of depression, moments of doubt, conflicts with people, and failures in witness. Yet, we must remember that faith gets lazy if all is well and good all of the time. As painful as it seems, James Fowler, in his book *Stages of Faith Development,* reminds us that our faith only grows when we confront a contradiction that requires us to expand our circle of trust. At best, we hobble toward holiness; but if we keep our insatiable thirst for God along the way, He will give us "grace against grace" to handle our contradictions. So often, during times of struggle, I find myself humming Hubert Mitchell's song:

He giveth more grace as the burdens grow greater;
  He sendeth more strength when the labors increase.
To added affliction He addeth His mercy;
  To multiplied trials, His multiplied peace.

His love has no limit; His grace has no measure.
  His pow'r has no boundary known unto men.
For out of His infinite riches in Jesus,
  He giveth, and giveth, and giveth again.

Hallowing Grace

Wesley's struggles are most evident in his search for joy in the fullness of the Spirit. He thought that he might find the answer among the Moravians who had been so instrumental in leading him to saving grace. Returning to their company, he disagreed with their insistence that the fullness of the Spirit came at once in the work of regeneration. If so, it meant that the experience of Aldersgate was canceled because with the fullness of the Spirit comes the sense of joy. Also, as we remember, Wesley began to pray immediately after Aldersgate for those who had abused and persecuted him. The mysticism of the Moravians lacked the social conscience that was stirred at Aldersgate for Wesley. Therefore, he turned aside from them. In his journal, we read of Wesley writing to his brother, Samuel, with the confession, "There is still in me the carnal heart."

Although the time and place of Wesley's sanctification is a matter of historical conjecture, there is no doubt but that he received the fullness of the Spirit as the gift of hallowing grace. His analogy of a house to characterize the full scope of the Christian experience is most enlightening. Repentance, he says, is the porch, justification is the doorway, and sanctification is the hallowing of all of the rooms of the house. I would only add that prevenient grace is the pathway leading to the porch.

So, whether in his writing, his sermons, his testimony, or his task, Wesley enlightens us to the joy that comes with the fullness of the Spirit—the joy that he missed at Aldersgate. How else can we explain the equation that he propounded, "Holiness is happiness"? How else can we account for his admonition, "Sour godliness is the devil's religion"? Most of all, how can we refute the hymn:

Breathe, O breathe Thy loving Spirit
  Into ev'ry troubled breast!
Let us all in Thee inherit;
  Let us find that second rest.

Take away our bent to sinning;
Alpha and Omega be.
End of faith, as its Beginning,
Set our hearts at liberty.

May God forgive us for making the experience of hallowing grace a point of theological controversy, a signal of spiritual superiority, or a stopping place along the road of our spiritual journey. Wesley would be the first to call us to grow toward the goal of the experience called "holiness" and never stop growing.

Wesley preferred to emphasize the "filling of the Spirit" rather than the "baptism of the Spirit." While he did not deny the gifts of the Spirit that are associated with the baptism, he felt as if the gift of the Spirit preceded the gifts of the Spirit. In a beautiful meditation called *The Theology of the Warmed Heart,* Frederic Platt reminds us what the fullness of the indwelling Spirit means. As Christ became flesh in the Incarnation, the Holy Spirit becomes incarnate in us through hallowing grace. Just as Christ emptied himself of His glory to become resident in human flesh, the Holy Spirit humbles himself to become resident in us. The apostolic ideal of being "filled with the Spirit" comes to life for us. Our human personalities become the "habitation of God by the Spirit."

Holiness is so practical and personal when we think of the experience this way. When the incarnate Spirit dwells in us, the motive of Christ's "perfect love" is possible. When the Spirit speaks through us, the Word of Christ is heard. When the Spirit moves through us, the grace of Christ is known. When the Spirit acts through us, the glory of God is revealed. As Platt writes, "He breaks within our souls the alabaster box of love exceeding precious, and the fragrance of it fills the house of life in which he dwells as eternal guest and minister." If so, the motive of perfect love is natural.

When we are filled with the Spirit of God, *He is the Helper of our infirmities.* Sharing our secret distress and our sorrows, He comforts us, removes the bitterness of our soul, opens our eyes, speaks peace through our turmoil, heals our wounds, makes us clean, and gives us strength.

When we are filled with the incarnate Spirit of God, *He also brings the Person of Christ into our dwelling.* He knows the anguish of our struggling nature; He suffers when we are despised, ignored, and rejected. He knows the insult of being an invited guest and ignored. Yet, He abides, patient even in suffering.

When we are filled with the incarnate Spirit of God, *He dwells in us with the peace and joy of Christ.* As the witness of the Spirit brings the joy of assurance, He also brings the joy of freedom—not bondage or fear.

When we are filled with the incarnate Spirit of God, *He intercedes for us.* In his meditation *The Theology of the Warmed Heart,* Platt goes on to explore the meaning of the incarnate Spirit dwelling in us and filling all our being. When I hurt, He hurts; when I ignore Him, He grieves; when I sin, He suffers; if I reject Him, the Son of God is crucified afresh. But at the same time, if I love, He loves; if I pray, He prays; if I preach, He preaches. Christlikeness is the proof of the Holy Spirit. Then, the peace of God through Jesus Christ is affirmed by rapturous joy. Charles Wesley captured the breadth and depth of these truths about hallowing grace when he wrote the hymn:

> O for a heart to praise my God,
>   A heart from sin set free,
> A heart that always feels Thy blood
>   So freely shed for me.
>
> A heart in ev'ry thought renewed
>   And full of love divine,
> Perfect and right, and pure, and good—
>   A copy, Lord, of Thine.

Giving Grace

Resting in the power and presence of His hallowing grace does not mean that we stop on our journey of faith. Immediately after Wesley experienced the heart strangely warmed, he began praying for those who had despised him and persecuted him. As Steve Harper writes in his book *Devotional Life in the Wesleyan Tradition,* piety and mercy are another inseparable link in the experience of holiness. So much so that Wesley defined the "witness of the Spirit" as a two-sided coin. On one side is the witness of the Spirit that we are the children of God—the inward evidence of piety. On the other side is the witness of the Spirit that we are obedient to His will—the outward evidence of mercy.

Giving grace is the final evidence of the Spirit-filled life. Jesus taught us the meaning of giving grace in the parable of the man who was forgiven of a major debt by the king but refused to forgive a brother who owed him a pittance. Consequently, the grace that he received was canceled by the king. To be fully operative, grace freely received must be grace freely given. Likewise, we cannot claim the fullness of the Spirit without showing the fruits of giving grace. Wesley passed this test. As proof of his sanctification, he was ready to go anyplace at any time and do anything for his Lord. Charles Wesley was so empowered by his brother's example that he pledged, "I would die with him."

We know that Wesley is credited with leadership in reforming a corrupt English society and saving the nation from bloody revolution. But we may forget the depth of that corruption and the magnitude of moral renewal. If so, let a best-selling work of history add a new dimension to our understanding. *The Fatal Shore,* by Robert Hughes, describes the conditions in 18th-century England prior to the Wesleyan revival. Debtors as well as hardened criminals were either hung in the public square or deported to the wilderness of Australia. As an opiate of the masses, public hangings were a spectacle of sport. Executions were usually three-day events. Coming early from far and wide to attend the sport, they roared out bawdy songs in gin houses with refrains like, "To be in deadly suspense." During the hanging itself the drunken mob laughed and ribbed the victim with the chants, "Dance upon nothing," "Take the earth bath," and "Shake a cloth in the wind." The masses were not alone in their callused view. Even Samuel Johnson opposed legislation to ban hangings as a public show by saying, "If they do not draw spectators, they do not serve their purpose."

Adding to this corrupted climate, the Restoration Theater produced the bawdiest of shows, a government lottery existed by cheating, corruption, and crime, public officials lived on briberies, and alcohol drugged the nation. In LondonTown, for instance, every sixth house was a pub. If the same ratio of drinking places were applied to the small town of Wilmore, Kentucky, with its 2,000 residents, there would be 120 bars to serve its citizens!

Against this climate of corruption, John Wesley lived out the fruit of the Spirit. Although he became one of the richest men in England, he lived annually on 28 pounds until his death, giving away the rest to the poor. On one occasion, at an advanced age, he walked for miles to a preaching appointment in order to save the carriage fare and give it to the poor. Both in personal discipline and social compassion, he lived out the triad of giving grace, "doing no harm, . . . doing good, and . . . attending all the means of grace."

Once again, we remember that John Wesley refused to become involved in the politics of the nation until Methodism had proven to be a redeeming influence in English culture. Then, and only then, did he step forward into the public eye to support legislation banning slavery, prohibiting child labor, and reforming prisons. Grace that is freely given will inevitably take us into the crucible of the public arena, but not before it has been demonstrated as a humble, sacrificial, and joyous expression of gratitude for grace that has been freely received.

TOGETHER ON THE ALDERSGATE ROAD

Aldersgate Street is a place. English political history records the fact that King James I marched through the narrow gate to establish his monarchy. English literary history tells us that Boswell lived there with his bride. The site on Aldersgate Street where John Wesley had his heart strangely warmed, however, is unknown. The best that Methodist historians can do is put up a plaque at the entrance to the street for visitors to see. If the exact site were known, we might be tempted to make it a shrine, worship the symbol, and lose the meaning of the event. Aldersgate is a marker event that cannot be duplicated in kind. Rather, it symbolizes a spiritual journey with marker events and continuing experiences.

Wesleyans are people together on that journey. On the road to Aldersgate, we are amazed at the evidence of God's leading grace; at a place called Aldersgate, we feel our heart strangely warmed by the power of saving grace, and on the road after Aldersgate, we are filled with the Holy Spirit through His sanctifying grace. All along the way, there is the assurance of our salvation. As a continuing question, Wesleyans ask themselves and each other, "Have you the witness of the Spirit that you are a child of God?" Wherever we are on the Aldersgate road, amazing grace lets us answer, *"Yes."*

3

One Holy Passion

"Wesleyans are a people with an insatiable thirst for God and a passion to be holy."

WESLEYANS ARE PEOPLE OF PASSION. First and foremost, we want to express our love for God by being known as a "holy people." Behind this all-consuming desire is our belief in the *doctrine* of holiness, our *experience* of a personal Pentecost, and our *practice* of holy living. Although the terms "holiness" and "entire sanctification" have been abused by debate and clouded by confusion, one thing is clear: Wesleyans are a people with an insatiable thirst for a God who calls us to be holy.

Once we understand Wesleyans as people with this passion, terms become incidental to the reality of the experience. Whether we are "filled with the Spirit," "sanctified by grace," or "purified by love," Wesleyans will not quibble. If faith is working through love in the experience of holiness and the practice of holy living, Wesleyans will be the first to say with the graciousness of their founder, "It is enough. Give me your hand."

Although Pentecost is cited as the momentous event that confirms God's desire for a holy people, sanctification is a strong Bible word with meaning throughout Scripture. What happens when a human being with an insatiable spiritual thirst comes into the presence of the Holy God? Let the prophet Isaiah tell us his own story, a story that mirrors our Wesleyan experience.

I. A GLIMPSE OF HIS GLORY

In the year that King Uzziah died, I saw the Lord seated
on a throne, high and exalted, and the train of his robe filled
the temple. Above him were seraphs, each with six wings:
With two wings they covered their faces, with two they covered their feet, and with two they were flying. And they were
calling to one another:
"Holy, holy, holy is the LORD Almighty;
the whole earth is full of his glory."
At the sound of their voices the doorposts and thresh-
olds shook and the temple was filled with smoke.

—Isa. 6:1-4

I remember the first sermon I ever preached. When I was 12
years old, there was a child prodigy featured in *Life* magazine
named "Little David" who traveled around the country preaching in
county fairs and camp meetings. Our local church pastor did not
want to be outdone, so he asked me if I would be his "Little David"
and preach a sermon. After having so many of the church ladies pat
me on the head and declare, "God wants you to be preacher," I had
no choice but to say yes. So, during the next Wednesday evening
prayer service, the pulpit was turned over to me for my first preaching experience. Like all first-time preachers who are honest, I bor-
rowed the outline for my sermon from the only source we had in our
home library. *Adam Clarke's Commentary* gave me my text from
Isaiah when the prophet "saw the Lord, seated on a throne, high and
exalted, and the train of his robe filled the temple" (6:1). Clarke also
gave me the kind of alliterative outline that preachers love with three
points: (1) The Awe; (2) The Agony; and (3) The Anointing.

More than 50 years of preaching have passed, but the memory
remains. While studying the Book of Isaiah in preparation for writing
two volumes of *The Communicator's Commentary*, I thought that my
search would take me far beyond the simplicity of that first sermon.
But no, the more that I read Isaiah, the more I realized that his vision
of God in the sixth chapter was the crux of the message for his day
and the need for our day as well. Moreover, as a Wesleyan with an insatiable thirst for holiness, I found myself reliving Isaiah's experience.
So, through the eyes of the prophet, I invite you to come with me into
the presence of the Holy God where we get a glimpse of His glory.

His Awesome Presence

Critics dispute the chronological placement of Isaiah's vision because it appears as if his call to be a prophet in chapter 6 came after
he had already prophesied throughout the first five chapters. For

those of us who know the reality of our own spiritual journey, however, Isaiah's vision takes on added meaning because of its placement.

In the first five chapters of the book, we learn that Israel had become too complacent in a time of peace to heed the warnings of God and too corrupted in a time of prosperity to escape the punishment of God. Not only that, but Uzziah, a good king for 52 years, had become arrogant, profaned the Temple, contracted leprosy, and died in shame. All Israel needed to be shaken by a vision of the Holy God, high and lifted up, sitting on a throne, with the train of His robe filling the Temple. Each of these symbols—the title "Lord," the throne, the lofty position, and the all-encompassing robe—attested to His sovereignty over all of the universe, over all of its kings, over all of their nations, and over all of its people, including His chosen children of Israel.

The Sovereignty of God. Isaiah's vision leaves no doubt about the sovereignty of God. Nations turn against Him, but His will prevails; kings compete with Him, but they fall in shame; people turn from Him to worship idols, but their false gods crumble. Even His chosen people refuse to trust Him, but they do not escape punishment. And, mystery of mysteries, a pagan despot named Cyrus becomes His instrument, but even he must pay for his sins. Yet, through it all, the sovereign Lord promises to preserve a remnant through whom the Savior will come to set up an ultimate reign when swords are beaten into plowshares and the lion will lie down with the lamb. Without the slightest doubt, Isaiah tells us that the sovereign Lord still writes the script of human history.

The Holiness of God. As a prophet, Isaiah accepts the sovereignty of God; as person, he needs to see His holiness. Sovereignty is the powerful nature of God; holiness is the moral character of God. He is pure; He is complete; He is whole.

R. C. Sproul, in his book *The Holiness of God,* notes that holiness is the only attribute of God that is presented in Scripture in the superlative. When His holiness is extolled by the seraphim in antiphonal chorus, they sing, "Holy, Holy, Holy." No other attribute is so praised. Angels do not sing, "Love, Love, Love" or "Justice, Justice, Justice." They only sing, "Holy, Holy, Holy."

We understand why the seraphim used their wings to cover their feet. Even without sin, they cannot stand to have the Holy God look upon their created nature. So, Coleridge wrote:

> *Weave a circle round Him thrice,*
> *And close your eyes with holy dread,*
> *For He on honey-dew hath fed,*
> *And drunk the milk of Paradise.*

He and He alone is holy.

The Glory of God. Isaiah sees the moral character of God expressed in His "doing" as well as His "being." In the imagery of the vision, we learn that wherever He touches down He leaves the ethical imprint of His glory. So, again the seraphim must hide their faces. As with all created beings, they cannot gaze upon the glory of God. Moses, we remember, asked God to see His glory. God answered, "I will cause all my goodness to pass in front of you, and I will proclaim my name, the LORD, in your presence . . . but . . . you cannot see my face, for no one may see me and live" (Exod. 33:19-20).

In Christ we see this truth personified. We read in Phil. 2:7 that He emptied himself of His glory in order to become a man and die for our sins. Yet, He left the imprint of His character in all that He did so that John could write, "We have seen his glory, the glory of the One and Only" (John 1:14). In further confirmation of the divine character of Christ, the writer to the Hebrews adds, "The Son is the radiance of God's glory and the exact representation of his being, sustaining all things by his powerful word" (1:3). But now for the best news of all. Even though we cannot gaze directly on the glory of God, we can share the glory of Christ. Becoming one with Him, we inherit the promise, "And we, who with unveiled faces all reflect the Lord's glory, are being transformed into his likeness with ever-increasing glory, which comes from the Lord, who is the Spirit" (2 Cor. 3:18).

Three profound truths emerge. In the *sovereignty* of God we encounter His will, which never loses its mystery; in His *holiness* we learn of His purity, which cannot tolerate sin; but in His *glory* we learn of His mercy, which promises a remnant out of which will come a Savior who will redeem all nations. No wonder that Isaiah heard the song of the seraphim, "Holy, holy, holy is the LORD Almighty; the whole earth is full of his glory." No wonder the posts shook and smoke filled the Temple. Isaiah was in the awe-filled presence of the Lord—sovereign, holy, and glorious.

Our Ambivalent Response

How do we respond to the presence of God? To His sovereign will? To His holy character? To His glorious works? Our children have the answer when they exclaim, "It's awesome!"

Awe brings out many responses, but one stands out above all. Before His sovereignty, we shut our mouths. In the presence of the Lord, the psalmist said, "I shut my mouth." The argumentative Job, too, encountered the sovereignty of God and confessed, "I put my hand over my mouth" (Job 40:4).

Rudolph Otto, in his book *The Idea of the Holy,* reminds us that we are ambivalent in His presence. Before the *mysterium* of His holiness, our response is *tremendum* and *fascinans*. We tremble with fear and awe, but at the same time we are fascinated by His holiness, which is attractive, desirable, promising, and compelling. So, with what Peter calls "reverent fear" (1 Pet. 1:17), we shut our mouths, cover our feet, and hide our eyes before the sovereignty, holiness, and glory of God.

His Transforming Promise

Just as Isaiah's character and conduct were transformed in the presence of the Holy God, our Wesleyan character and conduct begin in this awesome setting.

Here is where our *worship* begins. In his book *Reality in Worship*, J. P. Allen likens our worship to entering a planetarium from a busy, noisy street. Dimming lights hush the sounds, and the universe opens up over our heads. Earth becomes one of the smallest of planets, and we become one of its smallest creatures. In that awesome moment we focus upon the greatness, the goodness, the glory, and the grace of God. This is our standard for worship, whether the style is traditional or contemporary. Our focus is not upon ourselves and our needs, but upon the character of God. We are not to proceed at our own entertainment-driven pace, but to wait in His holy presence; not to assume that there is nothing new under the sun that we have not seen, but to come expecting a glimpse of His glory.

Here is where our *holiness* begins. Not only does the holiness of God call out the Christ who redeems us, but it also gives us the promise that we can be imprinted with His character. God's desire is that we be holy as He is holy. When we worship in reverent fear, we will follow after holiness in our character (2 Cor. 7:1) and walk circumspectly in our conduct (Eph. 5:15). Even now, I can hear Henry Clay Morrison, the founding president of Asbury Theological Seminary, telling the student body, "We are born again as God's children. Just as no honest father wants his son to be a thief, and no industrious father wants his son to be sluggard, and no upright father wants his son to be immoral, so God our heavenly Father, being holy, wants us, His children, to be holy like Himself."

As Wesleyans, here is our prayer:

> *Teach me to love Thee*
> *As thine angels love.*
> *One holy passion*
> *Filling all my frame.*
> *The baptism of the heaven-descended dove;*
> *My heart an altar,*
> *And Thy love the flame.*
> *Amen.*

II. OUR TELLTALE HEART

> "Woe to me!" I cried. "I am ruined! For I am a man of
> unclean lips, and I live among a people of unclean lips, and
> my eyes have seen the King, the LORD Almighty."
>
> —Isa. 6:5

Murder mysteries that came over the local radio station were
taboo in my boyhood home. Perhaps that is why I developed an early infatuation with the works of Edgar Allan Poe. Out of his drug
dreams came such prose as "The Cask of Amantillado" and such
poetry as "The Raven." Secretly, I absorbed them with the full scope
of my fantasy.

Among the short stories of Edgar Allan Poe, "The Telltale Heart"
is my favorite. As always, Poe himself is the culprit in a violent scene.
An old man who lives with him has a vulture eye with which Poe becomes obsessed. To escape the eye, Poe decides that he must kill the
old man. So, in the dark of night, he enters the old man's room, lets a
crack of light out of his lantern, and sees the vulture eye fixed on
him. As Poe toys brutally with his victim, the old man's heart begins
to pound, faster and louder. Then, when the old man screams, Poe
smothers him with a pillow to make sure that he is dead.

To cover his crime, the murderer takes up the planks of the living room floor and buries his victim. Suddenly, there is a knock on
the door. Police are there to check out the report that a scream
came from the house. Poe explains that he screamed in a nightmare
and invites them in for a cup of tea. As they sit in the living room,
Poe places his chair directly over the body of his victim. The policemen smile and chat as they drink their tea. What's that? Poe hears a
heartbeat, muffled at first and then rising to a staccato sound for all
to hear. Louder and louder it grows in his ears while the policemen
still chat and smile. Louder, louder, and louder it grows until Poe
shrieks, "Villains, dissemble no more! I admit the deed—tear up the
planks—here, here—it is the beating of his hideous heart!"

Despite his drug dreams, Poe comes close to a truth from which
we cannot escape. As he sat in the presence of the officers, the telltale heart revealed his guilt and exposed his sin.

Isaiah had a similar experience when he got a glimpse of the
glory of God. His first response was to bow in holy awe as the
seraphim sang:

> "Holy, holy, holy is the LORD Almighty;
> the whole earth is full of his glory."

Now we join Isaiah as he moves from awe to agony. In the presence of God he sees himself and weeps, "Woe to me! . . . I am ru-

ined!" It is the sin of our telltale heart that betrays us. Because Wesleyans are people who confront the full reality of human sin that is exposed before the holiness of God, our cry of "Woe" is always heard as we journey toward the experience of His anointing. We must be ready to confront three uncomfortable and unpopular truths.

Anguish for Our Sin

When we see the holy character of God, *we feel anguish for our sin.* Isaiah cries, "Woe to me! . . . I am ruined." Other translations add force to his words. One says, "Woe is me! I am lost" (NRSV) and still another intensifies the cry, "My doom is sealed" (TLB).

Whatever the cry, Isaiah is confessing that he is unworthy to join the seraphim in singing, "Holy, Holy, Holy."

The truth is fundamental. Whenever we see the King, the Lord Almighty, our sinfulness is exposed. Like the pounding of the telltale heart, we can only cry, "Woe is me!" Hugh Kerr and John Mulder have written a book titled *Conversions* in which they cite the verbatim testimonies of spiritual leaders from the apostle Paul to Charles Colson, with such notables as Augustine, Calvin, Bunyan, Wesley, Spurgeon, Tolstoy, William Booth, Schweitzer, C. S. Lewis, and Thomas Merton in between. Using Isaiah's vision of God as the model, the authors observe that in every conversion they studied, there is agony of soul, the stab of conscience, the shame of inward uncleanness, the remorse of sin, and the sensation of being lost and alone.

When John Bunyan, for instance, got a glimpse of the holiness of God, he reported that he felt like a child falling into a well-pit. Sprawled in the water at the bottom of the pit, he could find no handhold or foothold to lift himself out. He felt that he would die in that condition. From that memory comes the allegory of *Pilgrim's Progress.*

Søren Kierkegaard, another subject in the book, describes himself as a rower in a boat who tried to save himself by rowing frantically against the stream toward God. Finally, in exhaustion, he drops the oars and feels himself spinning without hope toward the brink of the falls.

Charles Colson describes his conviction for sin in his biography, *Born Again.* He tells of Tom Phillips, chairman of Raytheon, reading to him from C. S. Lewis's *Mere Christianity:* "In God you come up against something which is in every respect immeasurably superior to yourself. Unless you know God as that—and therefore, know yourself as nothing in comparison—you do not know God at all."

Colson confesses, "Suddenly, I felt naked and unclean, my bravado defenses gone. I was exposed, unprotected . . . Lewis' torpedo had hit me amidships. I saw myself as I never had before. And the picture was ugly."

Why do such testimonies sound strange and melodramatic to our ears? The answer is that our spiritual sensitivity to sin is dulled because we have lost sight of a holy God. Even our worship is sometimes nothing more than what Malcolm Muggeridge calls, "Agnosticism sweetened by hymns." Yet, the truth cannot be denied. When we enter the presence of God, in the vision of His holiness we see the ugliness of our sin. The vision must never be forgotten.

Responsibility for Our Sin

Another agonizing truth comes to us from Isaiah's response. When the prophet sees God, *he accepts responsibility for his sin.* "I am a man of unclean lips," or "I am a foul-mouthed sinner," allows for no exceptions and leaves no room for shifting the blame. Isaiah is saying that he has no place in the presence of God, no right to praise God, and no authority to speak for God.

Not without significance, Isaiah confesses that he is a man of "unclean lips." Jewish people saw lips as more than a specific set of sensory organs. To them, the lips spoke the motives of the heart and the decisions of the will. So, Isaiah is confessing that through his lips, his telltale heart has betrayed him. Jesus confirmed this truth when He said, "The things that come out of the mouth come from the heart, and these make a man 'unclean'" (Matt. 15:18).

For Isaiah, "unclean lips" had another meaning. In the first five chapters of the book, Isaiah had been pronouncing woes upon the nations that denied God. Now, when he gets a glimpse of the holy character of God for himself, he must ask, "How can I speak for God without a heart like God?" Every preacher, teacher, counselor, and witness for the Word of God must ask the same question. If there is sin in our hearts, our lips will betray us.

Jacques Ellul has written a book titled *The Technological Bluff.* In brief, he says that the advances of technology seem to promise unlimited progress and unlimited good. This is a bluff. Technology, as with all human achievements, has its downside. With the advancements comes a price to pay, a moral decision to make, and harmful consequences to consider. In the same vein, we are also victims of a theological bluff. This is the ruse that makes sin a nonfatal sickness for which someone else is responsible. In modern society, theology depersonalizes sin, psychology explains it, sociology excuses it, and economics pays for it. The time has come to call this bluff. As Isaiah teaches us, in the presence of God we and we alone are responsible for unclean lips that betray the sin of our telltale heart.

The Influence of Our Sin

From Isaiah's confession, we learn that sin has yet another dimension that we prefer to ignore. After confessing his own sin, Isaiah goes on to say, "I live among a people of unclean lips." Although sin is primarily personal, we cannot deny that our sin also has a social dimension. So when we see the holy character of God, we also see the pervasive influence of our sin. Unclean lips symbolize corruption at the very heart of the culture.

Another hard fact looms before us: *as leaders, we must accept responsibility for the sins of people.* In this context, the title of leader is not limited to persons with a formal role or title. Anyone who has followers is a leader. Whether presidents or parents, prophets or peasants, each of us is a leader because someone is following us.

We are well aware of the truth that the sins of the fathers are visited upon the children, but now we learn that the sins of the leader are visited upon the people. King David is a classic case (2 Sam. 24:10-17). When he sinned against God by counting his armies, he confessed, "I have sinned greatly in what I have done. Now, O LORD, I beg you, take away the guilt of your servant" (v. 10). So God gives David three options: three years of famine, three months of fleeing from his enemies, or three days of plague upon the land. David pleads, "Do not let me fall into the hands of men" (v. 14), and God sends a plague in which 70,000 die. When David realizes what he has done, he begs again, "I am the one who has sinned and done wrong. These are but sheep. What have they done? Let your hand fall upon me and my family" (v. 17).

In the presence of God, we see the sin not only in ourselves but also in others—our family, our congregation, our community, and our culture.

The Sound of the Telltale

Why all of this emphasis upon sin? Why not get on to the anointing of Isaiah? An answer came to me while reading about the role of the pastor in the Early Church. Two qualities served as the credentials for ordination in the apostolic succession. One was to be "blameless in character," the other was to be "true to the Word." Later on, ordination became an end in itself, so that even a scoundrel or a heretic could serve as the pastor ministering the means of grace. We need to return to the original model. Pastors as well as their people or anyone who carries the Christian witness must be "blameless in character" and "true to the Word." The two qualifications are inseparable. We cannot be true to the Word until we are blameless in character and vice versa. If there is any unconfessed sin in our lives, we are neither ready nor worthy of His anointing.

I love to play squash. It is a fast-moving game played with a stringed racket and a hard rubber ball on an indoor court. On the front wall of the squash court is a metal strip that rises 18 inches off the floor. The top of the strip is marked by a bright red line. It is called the "telltale" because if you hit the ball against the metal strip, you lose the point. In squash you do not have disputed calls about whether the ball is fair or foul as you do in other games. If you hit the telltale, there is an unmistakable metallic "twang" that betrays your fault and signals the lost point.

If we come into the holy presence of God with unconfessed sin in our heart, the same unmistakable sound of the telltale is heard. Try as we might, we cannot skip from the awe of His presence to the anointing of His Spirit without going through the agony of our sin. And if we have unconfessed sin in our hearts, sooner or later the telltale will sound and we will cry, "Woe is me! . . . I am undone" (KJV). Until we confess that sin, we are not ready for the cleansing touch of fire upon our lips.

III. FIRE ON OUR LIPS

"Then one of the seraphs flew to me with a live coal in his hand, which he had taken with tongs from the altar. With it he touched my mouth and said, 'See, this has touched your lips; your guilt is taken away and your sin atoned for'" (Isa. 6:6-7).

As Isaiah's vision of God moves to its conclusion, "fire" is the metaphor that commands our attention. In the image of a coal of fire upon Isaiah's lips, another truth comes forward as a condition of our holiness. If our cleansing is partial, if our spiritual consecration is dull, or if our spiritual commitment is shaky, God has a word for us in Isaiah's vision. The word is the same one that the philosopher Blaise Pascal used to describe his life-changing spiritual experience in 1654. In bold, capital letters, he wrote in his diary on the day of his cleansing, the word "FIRE!"

The Fire That Purifies Us

Fire is the only answer for the uncleanness that Isaiah saw within himself and his people after he glimpsed the glory of the Holy God. Any doubt about the reality and the fatality of human sin is erased in this image of cleansing fire. Only the white heat of a live coal taken from the altar of God can cleanse our guilt and atone for our sin.

An Act of Violence. We don't like to admit that our sin requires such an act of violence. An ad in the local newspaper carried the headline, "Will You Come Back to Church If We Promise Not to Throw the Book at You?" Underneath those words there was a large picture of an open Bible with the explanation, "In our church, we believe in a loving and forgiving God. Come and join us this Sunday when we open the Bible in worship." While the intentions may be good and the marketing clever, there is a sense in which the ad is false advertising. A live coal from the altar of God reminds us that behind the love that takes away our guilt and the forgiveness that atones for our sin is a Cross that extracted a cost no less than the life of the Son of God himself. No, we don't throw the Book at sinners any more than God throws the Book at us, but we cannot deny the depth and totality of our sin, which requires the violence of the Cross and the purging of fire if our guilt is to be taken away and our sin atoned for.

A Point of Vulnerability. Contemporary Christians are equally uncomfortable with the point of purging fire. In Isaiah's case, his lips were touched by fire. As a prophet who would speak for God, his lips had to be clean, and if they were clean, his whole being was clean. Here is another truth that we cannot ignore. Each of us has a point of vulnerability that Satan attacks and God redeems. For Job, it was his righteousness; for David, it was his lust; for Peter, it was his self-confidence; and for Paul, it was his zeal. In each case, the point of vulnerability is also the entry point for our sin or our sanctification.

When I was a senior at Asbury Theological Seminary, my sight was fixed upon a Ph.D. in pastoral psychology. Acceptances had come from both Boston University and the University of Southern California for admission to their doctoral program. Also, ministry offers had come from a church on the East Coast and a Christian college on the West Coast that would assure financing for our young family as I pursued the Ph.D. All my plans were on track until Dr. J. T. Seamands came from India to speak in chapel and finished with the question, "Is God calling you to India?" In that moment, the call came in a clash of wills. "Would I be willing to give up the doctorate and go to India as a missionary?"

I left the chapel under deep conviction and went home to our small apartment to do battle with God. The struggle continued through the day—my stubbornness against God's sovereignty, my ambition against His will. Finally, around three o'clock in the afternoon, I prayed, "Lord, Your will be done. If You want me to go to India, I'll be on the first plane out—even if I never get a Ph.D." Once He had my will, the Ph.D. came back into view with India always in the background. Perhaps this is why I have never suffered from the disease called "Ph.Deity." The degree stood at the entry point to my soul and became the symbol of my sanctification, to which I returned time after time whenever I came to a spiritual intersection.

Later, I heard about a similar prayer addressed to God at a conference for Evangelical Christian leaders in the 1940s. Bishop Myron Boyd of the Free Methodist Church knelt next to a woman whom he didn't know at the time. He couldn't help but hear her plaintive plea, "O God, let Billy come home to help me raise our children." A long pause followed with only the sound of sobs. Finally, a resolute voice prayed again, "O God, use Billy for Your glory even if I cannot have him home at all." My friend had heard the prayer of Ruth Graham in a sanctifying moment at the entry point to her soul.

There is much ado about the timing for our sanctification and the meaning of holiness. But there is common agreement among all traditions that the fiery cleansing of the Spirit must be total—sanctifying every aspect of our personality. Lloyd Ogilvie, chaplain of the U.S. Senate, preached a sermon titled "Fire Doors of Our Mind." He recalls being awakened in the middle of the night by a caller who told him that his church was on fire. Although the damage was limited, the fire marshal required that fire doors be constructed between the rooms to keep the fire from spreading to the whole building. In his sermon, Lloyd likens the fire doors in his church to the fire doors that we erect at entry points into the rooms of our heart. Our purpose is to keep the fiery Spirit of God from cleansing us completely.

Not only must we ask, "What is the personal point of entry to our souls where we need to be touched by fire?" but also we must pose the probing question, "Have we erected fire doors to certain rooms of our heart to keep the Spirit from making us wholly holy?" Until our lips are touched by fire and our whole heart is cleansed, we are not ready for God to speak to us.

The Fire That Ignites Us

> Then I heard the voice of the Lord saying, "Whom shall I send? And who will go for us?"
> And I said, "Here am I. Send me!"
>
> —Isa. 6:8

Once Isaiah had been totally cleansed by the purifying fire, he could hear the voice of God speaking to him with the fire of passion. The call itself is not special to Isaiah. Rather, we hear the call of God echoing through eternity to all generations, "Whom shall I send? And who will go for us?" Isaiah answers, "Here am I. Send me!"

Oswald Chambers put that call into proper perspective when he became conscious of the voice of God also saying, "I need you for My service, but I can do without you." The call is God's; the choice is ours. Once that voluntary choice is made, the fire of God ignites our soul as He did Oswald Chambers's, who testified of that moment, "Oh, my whole being is ablaze and passionately on fire to preach Christ."

Elton Trueblood, one of my spiritual and intellectual mentors, wrote a classic book titled *The Incendiary Fellowship.* He interprets Jesus' words, "I am come to send fire on the earth" (Luke 12:49, KJV), not as the Day of Judgment when sinners are consumed, but as the fire of the Spirit that ignited the disciples at Pentecost. This is the welcome fire that strangely warmed the heart of Wesley; this is the contagious influence by which Augustine portrayed the spread of Christianity, in which "one loving heart sets another on fire"; and this is what William Temple meant when he spoke of being ignited by the "positive energy of righteousness, a consuming flame of purity."

When Isaiah answered, "Here am I. Send me!" he put the poor stick of his humanity upon the flame of God and became part of an incendiary fellowship that would sweep the world. As Trueblood puts it so succinctly, "A good fire glorifies even its poorest fuel." There is hope in this response for all of us. When we say, "Here am I. Send me!" the poor stick of our humanity is ignited with the passionate blaze of His consuming Spirit.

Satan flees before people who give themselves as kindling to be ignited by the fire of God. In C. S. Lewis's *Screwtape Letters,* Uncle Screwtape instructs his nephew Wormwood on how to handle a new convert to Christ. After the white heat of his conversion begins to cool, Screwtape advises, "Make him acquiesce in the present low temperature of his spirit and gradually become content with it, persuading him that it is not low after all. In a week or two, you will be making him doubt whether the first days of his Christianity were not, perhaps, a little excessive. Talk to him about 'moderation in all things.' A moderate religion is as good for us as no religion at all— and more amusing."

When our lips are touched with a live coal from the altar of God, we are not only cleansed from our sin but also set aflame and consumed by the energy of the Spirit to fulfill Paul's word to the Romans, "Be aglow with the Spirit" (Rom. 12:11, RSV).

The Fire That Refines Us

He said, "Go and tell this people: 'Be ever hearing, but never understanding; be ever seeing, but never perceiving.' Make the heart of this people callused; make their ears dull and close their eyes. Otherwise they might see with their eyes and hear with their ears, understand with their hearts, and turn and be healed."

—Isa. 6:9-10

Almost every sermon on Isaiah's vision stops with the response, "Here am I. Send me!" There's a certain romance in these words, something like, "Join the Navy and See the World" or the Army slogan, "Be All That You Can Be." But we stop too soon. By assuming that Isaiah's response is the end of the story, we miss the full meaning of fire on our lips. It is this fire that refines us.

The message that Isaiah had to take to the people of Israel is a far cry from recruiting slogans. God says, "Go and tell this people" the truth that will cause them to stop their ears, close their eyes, and harden their hearts. In other words, they will refuse to hear, see, or understand that they might be healed.

Isaiah cries out again in anguish, "For how long, O Lord?" God answers, "Until My land is devastated, . . . until My people are exiled, . . . until My remnant is disciplined, . . . until only a holy seed remains in the stump of the once mighty oak" (6:11-13, author's paraphrase).

The romance is gone. Only the fire of unquenchable devotion remains. This is the hardest lesson of all. The final proof of our sanctification is not in an ecstatic sign or in our contagious passion; it is in our faithfulness to the will of God.

In our faithfulness we see the refining fire of God at work. Malachi gives us the picture of a crucible of silver ore being put in a white-hot furnace (3:2-3). As the heat is turned up, the impurities in the ore rise to the surface. The silversmith then patiently skims off the impurities until the silver is pure. Molten silver is then poured into a cast that has the shape of an exquisite and useful vessel. After cooling, the smithy hammers, chisels, and files off the rough edges. As the final touch, then, he rubs the metal with his own fingers until it has the glow of perfection.

Purified by fire, fashioned for use, and finished by God's personal touch—that is the process to which God is committed when He calls us. Because He is so faithful to us, we must be faithful to Him. Samuel Rutherford wrote in his diary, "Oh, what I owe to the fire, the hammer and furnace of my Lord Jesus Christ." Robert Browning put a similar thought into the prayer:

> My times are in Thy hand,
> Perfect the cup as planned.

I had to learn this lesson the hard way. At one time, I struggled with the decision about leaving the presidency of Asbury Theological Seminary to assume the presidency of the Christian College Consortium. It was a classic win-win choice. I loved both roles and saw the fulfillment of ministry in either one. In the midst of my struggle, I consulted with my friend, Dr. George Brusharber, president of

Bethel College and Seminary. I framed my dilemma in the question "What do you do when the call of God to a new ministry is clear, but you still don't feel right about a move?" Dr. Brusharber answered with Spirit-guided wisdom, "When God calls us, He also releases us." What an insight! Isaiah responded to the call of God by saying, "Here am I. Send me!" and received an assignment to preach a message that would not be heard, so naturally he asked, "How long, O Lord?" God came back with the answer, "Until I release you."

Isaiah had to watch his beloved Israel punished for its sins and disciplined for its unbelief until nothing was left but the smallest seed of hope. Yet, he remained faithful. The live coal from off the altar of God not only cleansed him wholly and consecrated him fully but also burned in him with unquenchable devotion until the holy seed of hope burst forth with prophetic visions of a Savior whose name is "Wonderful Counselor, Mighty God, Everlasting Father, Prince of Peace" (9:6). And because of the fire of his faithfulness, he foresaw the message of the Savior:

> The Spirit of the sovereign LORD is upon me,
>   because the LORD has anointed me
>   to preach good news to the poor.
> He has sent me to bind up the brokenhearted,
>   to proclaim freedom for the captives
>   and release from darkness for the prisoners,
>   to proclaim the year of the LORD's favor.
> —61:1-2

Faithfulness also let Isaiah see a vision of the future that is sculpted in a statue at the entrance to the United Nations building in New York City—a vision that is yet to be fulfilled:

> They will beat their swords into plowshares
>   and their spears into pruning hooks.
> —2:4

Faithfulness is not a virtue of our time. Commitments are rare, loyalty is unusual, and faithfulness is an exception. But not for Wesleyans who share the vision of God as seen by Isaiah. There will be many days when we will feel as if no one is listening to our witness. There will be other days when we feel like quitting. Still other days will have us searching for the smallest seed of hope. From the experience of Isaiah, however, we learn that the fire of unquenchable devotion is the final proof of our sanctification. Faithfulness is a fruit of the Spirit that comes with the touch of a live coal upon our lips.

One Holy Passion—it begins in awe as we see the holiness of

God; it moves to agony as we see the reality of our sin, and it leads to anointing as we are touched by fire.

As Wesleyans, our song is our prayer:

> *Refining fire, go through my heart,*
> *Illuminate my soul,*
> *Scatter Thy life through every part,*
> *And sanctify the whole.*
> *Amen and Amen.*

4 Spirit of Learning

"Wesleyans are a people who are lifelong learners with the Holy Spirit as Teacher."

THEOLOGICAL CONFUSION, POLITICAL CONTRADICTION, and personal chaos are threats to the integrity of our Christian witness in the 21st century. A tendency toward a "generic evangelical theology" in which biblical distinctives are lost in the desire to be acceptable to the contemporary mind is evidence of our theological confusion. The temptation to be aligned with partisan movements that have selective moral agendas or ignore the whole counsel of God exposes our political contradictions. And evidence that Evangelical Christians suffer the same problems, ranging from abuse to addiction, as the general population tells us that we are also victims of personal chaos.

Without apology, I believe that scriptural holiness defined in biblical and Wesleyan terms is a Spirit-guided corrective for our theological confusion, political contradiction, and personal chaos. This does not mean that Wesleyans are exempt from these problems or hold an exclusive answer to their solution. I do believe, however, that we bring to these issues a biblically based understanding of the teaching ministry of the Holy Spirit that is practical for today and creative for tomorrow. Our responsibility is to address these issues from a Wesleyan perspective as part of our contribution to the viability and vitality of our Christian witness in the 21st century.

As background for this claim, let Harry Blamires speak from the introduction to his book *Where Do We Stand?* "Today's boundary between Christian fidelity and treachery is no floodlit Berlin wall, set about with watchtowers and man-traps and patrolled by jealous guardsmen; it is a frontier barely recognizable on the terrain over which it runs."

To locate that frontier, he says that we must engage in map work, charting the terrain and drawing the dividing line between faithful Christian witness and apostasy.

A map is better than a rule book for guiding Christians through the "no-man's land" of a hostile culture. We have that map in the Word of God, which we believe to be the "only infallible rule for life and faith" (Lausanne Covenant) for every human generation and in all circumstances. According to the promise of Christ, it is the unique teaching ministry of the Holy Spirit who leads us in the task of tracing the map of revelation on the new frontiers of Christian fidelity and witness. Then, when the map of revelation is unfolded to guide our faith and life, it is the gyroscopic balance of the Holy Spirit that keeps us on center and heading in the right direction.

Wesleyan theology brings three qualitative emphases to the map work. *First, we see the work of the Holy Spirit as a dynamic experience* in which He not only cleanses us as a act of grace but enlightens us as a continuing process. *Second, we see the Scriptures as "God breathed" in their inspiration,* meaning that the living Word is interactive with the continuing revelation of truth through the mind of the Holy Spirit. *Third, we see ourselves as learners under the teaching of the Holy Spirit* as we submit our minds as well as our hearts to Him.

For these reasons, Wesleyans pay particular attention to the often-neglected promise of Jesus that the Holy Spirit, "Whom the Father will send in my name, will teach you all things . . . He will convict the world of guilt in regard to sin and righteousness and judgment . . . He will tell you what is yet to come" (John 14:26; 16:8, 13).

Futurists tell us that if education is to prepare students for living in the world of tomorrow, they must be taught the process of *synthesizing, norming, and futuring.* How providential! Synthesizing implies the question, "What is the central truth that gives meaning to human history and holds all truth together?" Is this not what Jesus means when He promises that the Spirit will guide us into all truth? Norming implies the question, "What is the moral standard by which human behavior is guided and judged?" Is this not what Jesus means when He promises that the Spirit will convict the world of sin, righteousness, and judgment? Futuring implies the question, "What is our hope for the future and what is our role in that hope?" Is this not what Jesus means when He promises that the Spirit of Truth will show us things to come?

As Spirit-guided people, then, our task is intellectual as well as spiritual. Paul prays that the Philippians' love may grow more and more in knowledge and sound judgment (Phil. 1:9). John Wesley, in his *Commentary* on the phrase "reasonable service" in Rom. 12:1, establishes the inseparable connection between reason and holiness. Of reason, he says that it serves us "both in laying the foundation of true religion, under the guidance of the Spirit of God, and in raising the superstructure. . . . It guides us with regard to every branch both of inward and outward holiness." In sum, Wesley is saying that if we are biblical and if we are Wesleyan, there is no separation between a warm heart and a right head. His brother Charles put that same conviction into a prayer that should come back to Wesleyans again and again as we enter the 21st century:

> Let us unite these two
> So long divided,
> Knowledge and vital piety.

I. "HE WILL LEAD US INTO ALL TRUTH"

Behind Jesus' promise that the Holy Spirit will "lead us into all truth" are three working principles that shape our Christian worldview.

First, our Christian worldview is centered in Jesus Christ. Gerald Ford, former U.S. president, loved to tell the story about the minister who paid a pastoral call on a farmer. As they sat on the farmer's porch, the minister looked out to a hillside where a forest fire had burned away all the foliage and vegetation. Noting a stand of scrub brush poking through the blackened soil, the minister commented, "It's not very attractive, is it?"

"You're right," the farmer answered, "it's not as pretty as it could be, but it holds the world together."

No question is more important than to ask a person, "What is the truth that holds your world together?" For a Christian, the unequivocal answer is "Jesus Christ." When He promises that the Holy Spirit will lead us into all truth, Jesus puts himself at the center of that truth. A Christian is a person who believes that all human history turns on the event of the Incarnation when Jesus Christ, the Son of God, became flesh in order to redeem us. No one else can be at the center. This fact is reinforced by Jesus' word that even the Holy Spirit will not speak of himself, but only of what He has heard Christ speak. He shows us only what Christ has shown Him and He leads us only into the truth that Christ has revealed to Him. It was this fact that led the apostle Paul to write to the Colossians, "In him all things hold together" (1:17).

For those of us who believe in Jesus Christ, this truth may seem obvious. Facts give us pause. At one time, there was common agreement among scholars that "all truth is God's truth." But in the 18th century, we entered into what is known as the Age of Enlightenment. Both theologians and philosophers moved God out of the center of the universe and Christ out of the center of truth. Presumably, the "enlightened" human mind took their place. Miraculous advances along with tragic consequences followed. Scientific advancements credited to the freedom of the human mind have dazzled us, but the moral consequences have confounded us. Even now, predictions of the future are turning upon scientific discoveries in chips, genes, and atoms. Chips run our computers, genes shape our humanity, and atoms fuel our systems. Without a center to hold all things together, however, these fields of knowledge are dangerously fragmented and specialized. Scientific advancements in chips, genes, and atoms speed ahead of their social and moral implications; scholars in specialized fields do not talk to each other; and students complete college degrees without any unifying truth in the curriculum. There is, however, a glimmer of hope. As new knowledge explodes on the scene of the 21st century, the inevitable connections between diverse fields of learning are being revealed. Although still ahead of their time, some far-sighted scholars are pointing toward a "unity of knowledge" that would, in effect, expose the fallacy of enlightenment thinking. But what will be the center that unifies all knowledge in the future? Some thinkers are trying to develop an impersonal concept of God that will serve their purposes. Others will still contend for a humanistic position. Both will fail. Unless God in Jesus Christ is the center of all truth, human knowledge will never hold together.

Second, our Christian worldview is comprehensive. James Orr, in his classic work *The Christian View of God and the World,* says that when we make our commitment to the centrality of Jesus Christ, we commit ourselves to much more. We commit ourselves to the Bible as the revelation of the nature of God, the interpretation of human history, and the prediction of human destiny. Blamires in his book *The Christian Mind* makes the same point. When we commit ourselves to the mind of Christ, he says, we will have a supernatural orientation through which we see the power of transcendent God at work in the world today. We will have a view of human nature that sees the reality of sin. We will have a sense of truth in which we hold in balance the doctrines of Creation, the Fall, the Incarnation, the Resurrection, and the Second Coming. We will submit to the authority of the Word of God for the direction of our lives.

More than our theological framework is involved. There are no advances in human knowledge or events in human history that are excluded from our comprehensive worldview. When I was a college freshman, my first course in theology was taught by Dr. James F. Gregory. To describe the work of the Holy Spirit in our lives, he took a thread from his blue suit and said, "If you take any thread from this suit and put it under a microscope, you will see that it has the tone and texture of the whole cloth." Applying his illustration, he went on to say, "That is how the Holy Spirit works in our lives. Every fiber of our being is true to the tone and texture of the Spirit-filled life." The same can be said for our Christian worldview. When Jesus promises that the Spirit will "lead us into all truth," He means that there are no facts, ideas, notions, values, opinions, discoveries, or events that are not made "captive to the mind of Christ" by the Spirit of Truth.

Third, our Christian worldview is creative. Even though our view of the world is centered in Jesus Christ and comprehensive of all truth, it does not mean that we have all of the answers or are exempt from surprise. To the contrary, our Christian worldview is continuously being re-created as the Holy Spirit teaches us how to process new information through spiritual discernment. At a national conference on Christian higher education, Bernard Ramm proposed that new information coming into our field may be processed in one of three ways. If the information is compatible with the Word of God, we integrate it into our Christian worldview. If it conflicts with the Word of God, we refute it with reasoned understanding after serious study. But if the new information is a mystery that is neither compatible nor conflicting with the Word of God, we hold it in abeyance as an imponderable that invites further investigation. In each case, the Holy Spirit is our Teacher, helping us discern how new information is related to our faith position.

Our Christian worldview is not threatened by anxiety about new information. Sometimes, we might be tempted to close the circle of knowledge with the assumption that we already possess "all truth." Such a thought is not only a fantasy but also biblically wrong. We must remember that Christianity is the only worldview that does not have to close the circle of knowledge. Our faith lets us be fallible. We can admit that we do not have all of the answers, but we know the God who is the source of all truth. Human systems do not have this privilege. Whether in science, philosophy, or religion, human systems must close the circle of knowledge. B. F. Skinner, the renowned psychologist, is an example. He believed that all human behavior can be predicted and controlled by the behavioristic mechanism of a physical stimulus and response. To prove his point, he wrote a novel called *Walden Two* in which he created a utopian world where all human behavior was perfected by controlling the stimuli and conditioning their response. At the close of the novel, Frazer, who is the mastermind of Walden Two, stands high on a bluff looking down over the perfect world that he has created. In the last sentence in the book, Skinner reveals the blind faith that he has in his theory by saying:

Frazer's not on his throne,
All's right with the world.

Because Skinner's view of the universe has no eternal dimensions and his view of humanity has no spiritual reality, he must close the circle of his world around his own feverish little ego, making it a god in itself.

Draw the contrast with our outlook as Christians. With the promise that the Holy Spirit will lead us into all truth, we know that knowledge is progressive and our understanding is developmental. Along a line of continuous and creative teaching, the Holy Spirit brings us the truth when we need it and when we are ready for it. Thus, in the struggle with new information, changing circumstances, and even intellectual opposition, we are both humble and hopeful. Christians in general and Wesleyans in particular should stand on tiptoe at the forefront of scholarship as we anticipate the new frontiers of truth to which the Spirit of Truth will lead us.

II. "HE WILL CONVICT THE WORLD"

Information is not morally neutral. The more information we have, the more complex are the moral decisions that we must make. While we may prefer the simplicity of either/or choices in a black-and-white world, the new age of information in the 21st century will not give us this luxury. Rather than simply sorting our choices into either/or categories, we will have to work along an ethical continuum that requires that we consider multiple options, anticipate contagious implications, and weigh far-reaching consequences. The burden will be too much for us unless we have the discerning mind of the Spirit of Truth. Jesus anticipates our need in His promise, "And when He [the Spirit of Truth] has come, He will convict the world of sin, and of righteousness, and of judgment: of sin, because they do not believe in Me; of righteousness, because I go to My Father and you see Me no more; of judgment, because the ruler of this world is judged" (John 16:8-11, NKJV).

In this promise Jesus gives us the essential elements of an ethical system for making moral decisions as Christians. An ethical system requires three parts: a standard for judging right and wrong; a sanction that affirms right and condemns wrong; and a consequence that rewards right and punishes wrong.

The change in public attitude toward premarital sex illustrates how an ethical system works—and how it breaks down. Not many years ago there was the standard, supported by a moral consensus, that premarital sex was wrong. Public opinion confirmed the standard by a sanction that affirmed young people who deferred sex until marriage and reproved those who failed to live up to the standard. Consequences reinforced both the standard and the sanction. Young people who participated in premarital sex lived with the fear of pregnancy, and those who became pregnant served as examples of the consequences of the broken standard. Then, in the 1960s, the standard was challenged by the Kinsey Report, the sanctions were lost in the moral revolution started at Woodstock and glamorized by the media, and the consequences were lifted by the pill. Today, in the public mind, premarital sex is accepted as an individual preference without social condemnation and little fear of pregnancy. An ethical system has broken down.

A vital function of the Holy Spirit is to teach us the ethics as revealed by Jesus Christ that undergird our Christian worldview. In the task of convicting the world of sin, righteousness, and judgment, the Spirit shows us the standard, sanctions, and consequences by which we are to judge right and wrong in human behavior and make our moral decisions.

First, our moral standard is belief in Jesus Christ. According to our scripture, sin is defined as the failure to believe in Jesus Christ. Behind this standard is the fact that our human nature rebels against God by rejection of Jesus Christ. The Holy Spirit's task is to convict the world of its sin and remind us that there is no other standard by which human behavior is judged.

To invoke belief in Jesus Christ as the moral standard for our Christian worldview may seem obvious to believers. But then, we remember that Kierkegaard once wrote, "If the Word of God said that everyone who believed was to receive a $100,000 gift, there would be no doubt about the clarity of the revelation and the promise. There would be no need for theologians to debate this truth, no need for commentaries to interpret it, and no need for seminaries to teach it. Everyone would believe the Word of God at face value." Perhaps with tongue in cheek, Kierkegaard then presses home his point, "The Word says with equal clarity that Jesus is Lord and there is no redemption other than in Him." Yet, "We establish theologians to study it . . . commentaries to interpret it and . . . seminaries to teach it."

Kierkegaard's provocative illustration reminds us why the Holy Spirit must teach us that belief in Jesus Christ is the standard against which our faith is judged. Even as Christians, we must confess that we secretly nurse the hope that our theologians, commentaries, or seminaries might find a way to hedge on this truth or fudge on its application to our own lives. As any faithful teacher, the Holy Spirit will repeatedly remind us that Jesus Christ, He and He alone, is Lord.

I remember an ecumenical setting in which 700 Christian college presidents gathered in a conference to discuss the future of their sector. Although all participants claimed the name "Christian" for their schools, their theology ranged from extreme liberalism to extreme conservatism with all stripes in between. Communion was planned for the opening session of the convention, and we all wondered how such a diverse group could ever come to a common table and partake of the Lord's Supper. The chaplain of one of the universities was in charge of the Communion meditation. We were amazed as he took the text, "No one can say, 'Jesus is Lord,' except by the Holy Spirit" (1 Cor. 12:3). At the close of his homily he invited all participants to join him at the Communion altar with this confession, "Jesus is Lord. We may say more, but we cannot say less." I, an Evangelical Christian, went forward to kneel between colleagues who were far apart in theology, but under the leading of the Holy Spirit, we were one in the confession, "Jesus is Lord."

Second, our moral sanction is righteousness through Jesus Christ. The second moral function of the Spirit of Truth is to convict the world of the meaning of righteousness as revealed in the life of Jesus Christ. As always, the focus is on Jesus Christ, who says that He is going to His Father and we will see Him no more. Yet, through the agency of the Holy Spirit, He leaves us the image of righteousness. Through this image, the Spirit of Truth teaches us what is right and what is wrong.

If I were asked to name the 10 books that have had the most influence upon my life, I would put close to the top of the list Charles Sheldon's novel *In His Steps.* As a teenager seeking to know the will of God, I shall never forget the question the characters in the book chose as the guide for all of their life decisions: "What would Jesus do?" Time and time again, I have asked that question when confronted with moral choices, large and small. Without fail, the question has taken me deeply into the mind and spirit of Jesus Christ. More often than not, the Holy Spirit brings from my memory an event or teaching from the life of Jesus that becomes a safe and sure guide for my decision.

Although criticism has been directed against the commercial venture of Christian bookstores that sell jewelry, bookmarks, and mementos by the millions that are engraved with the letters "WWJD" standing for the question "What Would Jesus Do?" we cannot fault the truth of the words because it is consistent with the work and teaching of the Holy Spirit. Whether dealing with issues of fact or opinion, ideas or values, code of conduct in our daily behavior, our first question must be, "What is the moral standard upon which our decisions are based?" The Holy Spirit will convict us if we embrace any standard that is not compatible with the mind and Spirit of Jesus Christ.

Third, our moral consequence is judgment by Jesus Christ. The Spirit of Truth will convict the world of judgment "because the ruler of this world is judged" (John 16:11, NKJV). We must be constantly reminded that all humankind is accountable to God. The cross of Jesus Christ is the symbol of His judgment upon sin and Satan. In the Cross, there is full freedom from the condemnation of sin, but there is also the continuing judgment upon the works and ways of every individual and institution on earth.

As our Teacher, the Holy Spirit saves us from arrogance by reminding us that all of our works stand under the judgment of God. Christians who believe that they are doing the work and will of God especially need this humility. Our best efforts are usually flawed by mixed motives and limited understanding. Therefore, the Holy Spirit will not let us take ourselves too seriously. Karl Barth was known as the "laughing theologian" because he saw how ludicrous it was to presume that we had all of the answers to the questions that theologians ask. His humorous outlook would be complemented by the witty scholar who said, "I wanted to be a theologian, but cheerfulness kept creeping in."

Frankly, I am suspicious of Christians who are so convinced of their faith or so compelled in their ministry that they cannot laugh. John Stott, at the 1974 World Congress on Evangelization in Lausanne, Switzerland, cut through all of the human plans for winning the world by telling the assembly that we are only commissioned to preach the gospel to the lost; it is the Holy Spirit who is responsible for the results. Not only is the ruler of this world judged by the cross of Jesus Christ, but our Teacher will not let our works of righteousness make us wise in our own conceits. Humility is the companion of honesty as we submit ourselves to the checks and balances of the Holy Spirit.

III. "HE WILL SHOW US THINGS TO COME"

Our Christian worldview must include an exciting vision of the future in which we see ourselves playing a significant part. Jesus promises to give us that vision through the work of the Holy Spirit who will tell us "what is yet to come" (John 16:13).

Secularists do not have that vision. Study after study of the general public, and youth in particular, culminate in an anxious mixture of hope and fear about the future. They find hope in their own self-confidence but fear that society is breaking down. Specifically, they lack confidence in our social institutions as agents of change and nurse the fear that they themselves will become victims of violence. Lest we as Christians be infected by this same anxious fear, we must ask, "What is the vision of hope for Christians in the world of tomorrow?"

We are now in a minefield set with apocalyptic, eschatological, and teleological or "end-time" traps. Although all Christians look forward to the time when Christ's purpose will be fulfilled on earth, we quickly divide and fight over the details. Only the Holy Spirit can help us work our way through the minefield and draw a map for others to follow.

Return to the image of the Holy Spirit as a gyroscope. The more powerful the contending forces and the faster it turns, the better balanced the gyroscope becomes. So, as we apply the analogy to the Holy Spirit as our Teacher, we see how He balances contending forces and gives us hope for the future.

First, the Holy Spirit balances our short-term and long-term view of the future. There is no question about the fact that Christianity is a long-term view. By definition, a secular society is limited to the short-term view of this present age.

Barbara Ward spins an evolutionary fable in her book *Spaceship Earth*. The fable begins with a bird fishing in shallow waters during the time of the Ice Age. This bird has a long beak so that it can stand in the shallows waiting for fish to come and spawn. With the long beak, it can dip into the water, snatch a fish, and enjoy a meal. But then, the fable continues. As aeons of time pass, the ice cap begins to melt and the waters begin to rise. Evolutionary theory imagines that the bird adapts to its environment by growing a longer beak in order to catch fish in the rising water. During this time, the bird never has to fly because there are always plenty of fish to eat. The waters continue to rise and the beak grows longer and longer. Finally, the time comes when the waters are too deep and the bird realizes that it must find new shallows in order to survive. Trying to fly, the bird finds its wings too weak and its beak to heavy to get off the ground. According to the fable, this is how the dodo bird came to be.

Ward's fable has a lesson for us. She concludes that we can spend so much time in the specifics of the present that we lose our ability to foresee the future and make the adjustments needed for changing times. Here is where the Holy Spirit becomes our mentor. He will keep us on alert against the seductive, short-term satisfactions of a secular society. Better yet, He will not let us lose sight of the long-term view that God wants us to see.

The other extreme is to become so fixated on the future that our spirituality becomes mystical and impractical. Rather than becoming immersed in the secular society, we become isolated from it. Here again, the Holy Spirit serves as our mentor in the balancing out of the short- and long-term view. In that delicate balance we are neither immersed in the secular society nor isolated from its issues. Rather, we are to become what Richard Niebuhr called "critical participants" in our culture. At one and the same time, we are to be involved in the social and moral issues of our society while maintaining the objectivity of our faith position. When Jacques Ellul describes the role of Christians in a rotting, urban culture, he says that we must work for change while being ready to flee at any time. Each of us needs the mind of the Spirit of Truth in order to balance out our short-term steps with our long-term vision. As our Teacher, the Holy Spirit shows us how to live productively, playfully, and purposefully.

Second, the Holy Spirit balances our pessimism and our optimism for the future. Again, the primary truth is that Christianity is guided by the optimism of the "Good News." Consistent with God's redemptive plan, our long-term vision sees the transformation of the earth and the consummation of time in the new creation, the new order, and the new kingdom (Isa. 65:17-25).

But there are extremes. Harvey Cox, in his book *The Secular City,* claimed that the secular mind and spirit represent the maturing of the creation story in which man increases and God decreases. Cox went on to claim that the Great Society of the 1960s represented the fulfillment of the liberal vision for a Christian century and might even represent the Second Coming. After watching the failure of the Great Society in the 1970s and the rise of political conservatism in the 1980s, however, Cox reneged on his earlier position and admitted that his glowing optimism about our secular society was obsolete. He illustrates the quip that a neoconservative is a liberal who has been mugged by reality.

Pessimism can also creep in. Futurists ride the waves between giddy optimism and fatalistic pessimism. Christians can get caught up in the same extremes. Some Christians have already pronounced doom on our society, and others see the evidence of Armageddon in every sign of world events. When I wrote the book *The Coming Great Awakening* in which I foresaw the prospects for spiritual revival at the end of our century, I based my text on the promise of Joel that Peter used as his text for the sermon at Pentecost, "In the last days, God says, I will pour out my Spirit on all people" (Acts 2:17). Talk shows that followed after the publication of the book revealed that many Christians believe we are living in the last days but see no hope of spiritual recovery. Through the tunnel vision of pessimism they see the prophecy of sin but do not see the promise of grace.

In Billy Graham's book *Approaching Hoofbeats: The Four Horsemen of the Apocalypse,* he tells the story of being in a French art museum with his wife, Ruth. On the wall was an impressionist painting by Renoir. Billy walked up to it and observed, "I can't understand this smear on the wall." Ruth told him, "Billy, you're too close. Stand back and you'll see the pattern." Applying that lesson to reading the Book of Revelation, Graham says that we must step back in order to see the pattern.

John the Revelator lets us know what it means to step back when he introduces his futuristic text with the words, "On the Lord's Day I was in the Spirit" (Rev. 1:10). Through the mind of the Spirit, we see things to come in the balance between the reality of human sin and the promise of God's grace. In that balance, we are called to be realistic optimists.

Third, the Holy Spirit shows us the balance between process and event in our view of the future. No one doubts that Christianity is known by its events. As we look back to the Incarnation as the turning point in human history, we look forward to the second coming of Christ as the culminating event in human redemption. Carl Henry, in his book *God, Revelation, and Authority,* notes that the key difference between Christianity and other worldviews, such as secularism, humanism, or scientism, is that Christians believe in what he calls a Final Personal Cause of which the Second Coming is a part. By denying a Final Personal Cause, the worldviews of secularism, humanism, and scientism focus on process without an event that will culminate their search.

For Christians, the greater danger is to focus on the event at the expense of the process. When I was a senior in high school, a traveling evangelist came to our holiness tabernacle with the billing as "The Professor of the Pyramids." This self-proclaimed doctor and professor brought a large, multicolored chart and a long pointer to the platform with him. On the chart was the cutaway drawing of the Great Pyramid in Egypt. With a dramatic flourish of the pointer, the professor identified the entryway as the symbol of Creation and the downward shaft as proof of the Fall. Through the narrow passageways and into the chambers he went with his pointer, tracing by length and space the stages of human history. Finally, he came to a very narrow passageway that he described as the "Age of Reason or the Age of Enlightenment." Then bursting into the secret chamber where the treasures of Tut were found, he shouted, "This is the Second Coming!" You can imagine the impression that he made upon his congregation as he took out his ruler, measured the length of the final passageway, counted the time of the centuries, and then announced with the precision of a scientist, "Jesus Christ is coming again on April 21, 1947!"

Of course, the professor's declaration led to an altar call. Because the meeting took place sometime in March 1947, he had urgency on his side. I went forward to the altar, not praying for salvation, but asking God to delay His coming until I could graduate from high school in June!

The story of the professor illustrates the fact that we can become so fixated on the event of redemption that we forget our responsibility for the process of redemption. Jesus said, "Occupy till I come" (Luke 19:13, KJV). E. Stanley Jones had the responsibility to write the strategy for the International Missionary Council in 1938. After hearing the debate on the coming kingdom of God, Jones wrote, "We work and we wait." His words are both biblical and Wesleyan. Following the command of Jesus and being taught by the Holy Spirit, we find the balance between event and process when "we work and we wait."

IV. "IN LOVE WITH THE TRUTH"

We have come full cycle on the meaning of Jesus' promise for the coming of the Spirit of Truth to be our Teacher. Parker Palmer, in his book *To Know As We Are Known: A Spirituality of Education,* tells us that the word "truth" is derived from the word "troth"—not unlike the pledge of two lovers who give themselves to each other. If then we want to know the truth, we must be betrothed to the Spirit of Truth. As Palmer writes, we are in "a relationship between the knower and the known—with which we are intimately bound in relationship forged of trust and faith."

As people known for our dedication to lifelong learning, Wesleyans must be pledged to the Spirit of Truth and betrothed in a relationship of trust and faith with Him. With the Holy Spirit as our Teacher and with our engagement to Him, our Christian worldview will be formed around three foundational truths in which we believe without reservation:

- All knowledge is the knowledge of Jesus Christ, for in His incarnation all things hold together.
- All morality is the morality of Jesus Christ, for in His cross all things are judged. And,
- All future is the future of Jesus Christ, for in His resurrection all things have hope.

Perhaps as never before, the 21st century will put these truths to the test. Even now, we are being bombarded by so much information from the media that we have trouble sorting out truth from fiction and falsehood. *How do we discern the truth?*

Adding to our dilemma is the fact that the flood of information is bypassing our traditional sources, namely preachers and teachers, upon whom we counted to help us interpret what we see and hear. Instant communication comes directly to us with a demand for a decision. *How do we decide for the truth?*

Most difficult of all, the information that overwhelms us is controlled by secular and commercial sources that are not friends of our faith. Admitting that the information we receive is being manipulated, we now talk easily about the "spin" on the news and accept "spinmasters" as part of the process. *How do we stand for the truth?*

No answer will suffice for these questions except as we become students under the teaching of the Holy Spirit. We must experience His cleansing fire, receive His enabling power, and learn His discerning ways. Holiness, in the Wesleyan context, embraces all of these dimensions of grace. To be "filled with the Spirit" is not only emotional but also intellectual and volitional. This is what it means to be "wholly Holy." Not one of these attributes of the Spirit can be out of balance in the 21st century. In the past, we have emphasized the ecstatic signs of our feelings or the rigid disciplines of our will. Consequently, some critics have put Wesleyans at the forefront of the anti-intellectualism of which the Evangelical movement has been accused. Their charge is unfair, but refutation is a waste of time. We must look forward.

True to our engagement to the Spirit of Truth, our task is to bring biblical balance back into the experience of the Spirit-filled life. Without neglecting our feelings or our discipline, we must meet the challenge of the information age with the mind of the Spirit. We accept Charles Malik's clarion call that we have the twofold task of winning souls and winning minds. We also respond to Elton Trueblood's plea that we must "outthink the opposition" in every generation.

If we are true to our biblical trust and our Wesleyan heritage, we will be known in the 21st century as reasonable and disciplined enthusiasts under the teaching of the Holy Spirit.

5

Heart of Compassion

"Wesleyans are a family of faith bonded together as one in spirit with open arms to embrace the stranger."

WESLEYANS ARE A FAMILY OF FAITH with many connections in their relationship. Foremost is the bond of *biblical theology* experienced and practiced in distinctive Wesleyan ways. Close behind comes the common expression of *Wesleyan worship* in which the joyous freedom of the Spirit is made strong by the solemn order of the creeds and the sacrament of the Lord's Supper.

The connections continue in a singular commitment to the *spiritual disciplines* that identify Wesleyans as "Methodists." Central to these disciplines is the personal practice of prayer, Bible study, solitude, and fasting along with membership in a small group for mutual support, learning, and accountability. Coming together, then, as a corporate body to seal these connections, Wesleyans follow a core of *governing principles* that give voice and vote to laity as well as clergy, women as well as men, local churches as well as larger jurisdictions, and internationals as well as nationals. Although some Wesleyans continue to follow the episcopal pattern of governance inherited from Wesley himself and others ascribe to congregational governance, the breadth of voice and vote is a biblical conviction for all.

Less formal but no less important connectors for the Wesleyan family are *matters of the Spirit.* Leading the way is what John Wesley called "a desire to flee the wrath to come." Anyone who made this confession was welcomed with open arms into the Methodist family.

Once introduced and converted to Christ, the new believer was nurtured toward maturity by the unifying question, "Have you the witness of the Spirit that you are a child of God?" An affirmative answer not only strengthened the common bonds of the family but advanced the believer into a spirit of compassion for the poor by which all Wesleyans were known. Far more than structure, *Wesleyans are one family together in the Spirit.*

If the trends that are accelerating and magnifying into the 21st century are accurate, our oneness as a Wesleyan family is due for a strenuous test. Already, we have seen the "connectionalism" of the Wesleyan movement put to test in doctrine, worship, and governance. The result has been a negative influence called "pluralism," which is nothing more than a politically correct code word for theological compromise. Now, in a world of increasing diversity of race, sex, age, ethnic origin, economic standing, educational achievement, social class, and cultural background, we face a new test. The question is whether or not the Wesleyan family will continue to be bonded by our desire to flee the wrath to come, our witness of the Spirit that one is a child of God, and our sacrificial compassion for the poor.

As a start on answering that question, we must contend *Wesleyans are a close-knit but not closed family.* Our inheritance is a family bonded together in the strength of love, but always leaning out with compassion for others and with wide-open arms to bring different and disenfranchised newcomers into the circle. In too many instances, we seem to be going in the opposite direction. Growing churches that recycle transitional people by appeals to those who are like-minded in class or color are promoted, local churches that cultivate parochial views of the world are touted, and small groups that close their ranks to outsiders are put forward as models.

Our purpose is not to criticize the church or its ministry but to ask a key question for the 21st century, *"Is the family of God ready for new and different members—'have-nots' as well as 'haves' and 'unlikes' as well as 'likes'?"* Little in our recent history tells us that we are ready. The results of a follow-up study on Billy Graham's New York Crusade in 1961 are often quoted. Although the decisions for Christ made by hundreds of people were genuine, a small number of them became involved in local churches. The study showed that the local churches had no open doors through which new believers could walk to become members of the family.

Our attitudes and actions must change if the church is to keep pace with the changing face of the future. A return to the biblical view of the family of God will make the difference. In his book

Reaching Out, Henri J. M. Nouwen reminds us that "hospitality" toward strangers is one of the three spiritual movements that demonstrate our faith to the world. Christine Pohl, professor of church and
society at Asbury Theological Seminary, adds scholarly strength to
Nouwen's insights in her doctoral dissertation by tracing "hospitality" through the Scriptures as evidence of grace received. For example, in giving the details of the Law to the children of Israel, God
gave the command, "The alien living with you must as treated as
one of your native-born. Love him as yourself, for you were aliens in
Egypt. I am the LORD your God" (Lev. 19:34). Job referred to this
command when he defended his righteousness by claiming, "No
stranger had to spend the night in the street, for my door was always
open to the traveler" (Job 31:32). Jesus, then, brought this commandment to fulfillment in His preview of the Last Judgment when
He invited His faithful servants into the presence of the Father with
the commendation, "For I was hungry and you gave me something
to eat, I was thirsty and you gave me something to drink, I was a
stranger and you invited me in, I needed clothes and you clothed
me, I was sick and you looked after me, I was in prison and you
came to visit me" (Matt. 25:35-36). Nowhere in Scripture do we
read that the commandment has been canceled. Under grace, however, the law becomes a privilege.

OUR BIBLICAL MODEL

The apostle Paul had one of the most delicate diplomatic tasks of
all time when he had to reconcile the mutual hostility between Jews
and Gentiles, unify them as "one in the Spirit," and bond them together as the family of God. When the crisis peaked in the Ephesian
Church, Paul wrote the inspired words that we need to reclaim for the
Wesleyan family in the 21st century. "For this reason I, Paul, the prisoner of Christ Jesus for the sake of you Gentiles—Surely you have
heard about the administration of God's grace that was given to me
for you, that is, the mystery made known to me by revelation . . . This
mystery is that through the gospel the Gentiles are *heirs* together with
Israel, *members* together of one body, and *sharers* together in the
promise of Christ Jesus" (Eph. 3:1-3, 6, emphasis added).

What we take for granted, Paul describes as a mystery and a
miracle. For him, to bring Jews and Gentiles together into a family
as coheirs, coworkers, and cobeneficiaries is the very clue to God's
plan for the ages. He goes on to say that family of faith that brings
Jews and Gentiles together is the most powerful witness of the

Church before rulers and authorities of both earthly and heavenly realms (Eph. 3:10).

How do we apply the meaning of this scripture to our polyglot of cultures in the 21st century? As Paul set these working principles for Jews and Gentiles in the Ephesian church, he would invoke them in his message to us. Being "heirs together with Israel" gives us our sense of *belonging* to the family of faith: being "members together of one body" gives us the *security* of the family of love; and being "sharers together in the promises of Christ" assures of being in a family of *hope* (Eph. 3:6). Faith, hope, and love are the building blocks of the biblical family and the signs that we are "one in the Spirit" together and with Christ.

I. Joint Heirs of the Faith

As "heirs together with Israel," Paul says that despised Gentiles are adopted into the family of God by faith. The Jews, of course, were God's chosen people. The relationship was sealed in a sacred covenant when God said, "I will . . . be your God, and you will be my people" (Lev. 26:12).

To think that we who are Gentiles could ever be included as God's chosen children with Israel is beyond human comprehension. No wonder that Paul spoke of a mystery and miracle. One needs only to experience the deep-seated hostility that still divides Jews and Arabs in Israel to understand what Paul meant. While the Jews and Arabs were negotiating a historical peace agreement to return land on the West Bank to the Arabs, my son Rob and I were visitors in the Holy Land. We made the mistake of flying out of Cairo, Egypt, to Tel Aviv, Israel. A slight glitch in our tickets resulted in being detained and under interrogation by Israeli security for more than an hour because we were two men traveling together as freelance tourists without all of the credentials and receipts that follow the typical tour group. In the Holy City we encountered the ancient hostility between Jews and Arabs again and again—in the sectioning of the city, in the division of holy places, and in the intrusions between the sectors as both sides vied for dominance. We also followed firsthand the zigzag lines of the map that showed how the peace agreement would chop up the land into little sections of Israel and Palestine so that visitors would have to go through two, three, or more international checkpoints every few miles.

Imagine trying to reconcile Jerusalem Jews and Palestinian Arabs as joint heirs in the same family. Yet, it happened! Paul knew it personally as a Jew as rabid as Zionist zealots of today. With holocaust in mind, he had taken on the responsibility for the "ultimate solution to the Christian question." Instead, after his encounter with Christ, he became the apostle to the Gentiles and even went so far as to alienate his fellow Jews by proclaiming the truth that the outcasts were "heirs together with Israel" as the people of God's covenant. He didn't stop there. The foundational principle for building a family of faith is extended with the announcement, "There is neither Jew nor Greek, slave nor free, male nor female, for you are all one in Christ Jesus. If you belong to Christ, then you are Abraham's seed, and heirs according to the promise" (Gal. 3:28-29).

Are we ready to come together as the family of faith according to these terms in the salad bowl of the 21st century? Neither Jew nor Gentile, male nor female, neither black nor white, neither young nor old, neither native nor immigrant, neither rich nor poor, neither advantaged nor disadvantaged, neither Catholic nor Protestant, neither Evangelical nor mainline, neither married nor single, neither Pentecostal nor Wesleyan, neither nationals nor internationals—all of our differences disappear in the common confession of our trust in Jesus Christ. Here, the mystery deepens. How can we retain the rich variety of our individuality at the same time that we are transformed on the common ground of faith? It is not easy. Our natural momentum is toward self-interest, which will fragment us. Only as we remember that we are the children of God, natural or adopted, with the same heritage of faith, can we be *"e pluribus unum"*—unified and diversified at one and the same time. On that common ground, reconciliation takes place and family begins.

II. MEMBERS OF ONE BODY

It is one thing to accept outsiders into the family and another thing to give them full voice and vote in family decisions. When Paul speaks of Jews and Gentiles coming together as "members of one body," he is introducing a revolution in the governance of the family. Imagine a peace agreement between Israeli Jews and Palestinian Arabs in our day including the provision for equal representation in their respective houses of parliament and with equal votes in policy decisions. Without grace, such a move is almost impossible.

My first project after retirement from the presidency of Asbury Theological Seminary was to update the history of the Free Methodist Church under the title *A Future with a History: Our Wesleyan Witness.* During the course of research and writing I became acquainted with statistics that showed that revival in the overseas church had swelled their numbers to three times the membership of

Free Methodists in the United States. Behind those statistics, however, were the stories of persecution and martyrdom as companions of revival. African leaders spoke in somber tones about their brothers and sisters who had been imprisoned, maimed, or killed for the sake of the gospel. But they didn't dwell on their persecution. Invariably, the look in their eyes changed from sadness to sparkle as they witnessed to the faithfulness of God in bringing thousands of their neighbors into the Kingdom. For me, it was a revelation. As we talked, prayed, and wept together, I repented of an attitude that protected me from their plight and kept me from embracing them emotionally and spiritually as full members of our Church who were just as close as my longtime friends in the next pew at home.

No longer can I trip off my tongue Paul's phrase—"members together of one body"—without opening up all of the implications of love for my overseas brothers and sisters. After completing the chapter on world missions as a record of history, I found myself weeping again as I put my newfound love into the rhythm of verse:

Lest We Forget
With tears we remember:
Our brothers and sisters
Who have fled as refugees
By the thousands;

Our pastors, lay leaders,
Spouses and children
Who have died as martyrs
By the hundreds;

Our bishops and church leaders
Who have been driven to exile
By the score;
Their blood and our tears
Write the heart of our history
At the end of the 20th century.

Two questions drive right to heart and soul of any organization or movement. "What do we celebrate?" and "Over what do we weep?" We know what Wesleyans celebrate when we sing the joyous hymns of grace. Such a quick answer does not come when we ask about our weeping. Few of us weep over lost souls, and fewer of us weep over suffering brothers and sisters overseas. Yet, if we are to live in a "global village" in the 21st century and claim that the "world is our parish," we must show what it means to embrace all

Wesleyans as "members together of one body." We know how to celebrate; we must learn to weep.

III. SHARERS TOGETHER IN CHRIST'S PROMISE

We have seen that it would take a miracle of grace for Palestinian Jews to include Arabs as coheirs of the faith once delivered to the children of God. We have also learned that it would take a greater miracle for the Jews to give Arabs full voice and vote in the governing councils of their synagogues, cities, and nation. The greatest miracle of all, however, would be reserved for the Jews to invite the Arabs to share the resources of God's promise—seeing the vision of Christ, receiving the grace of Christ, and anticipating Christ's hope for the future. Only a major miracle of grace can do that.

The word "sharer," or "partaker," in Paul's letter to the Ephesians is the word that calls out the image of a family dinner. Sitting down at a large, communal meal together is the reference point. To "share" implies a willingness to reduce your own portion so that all may be served.

When my wife, Janet, and I were married, we chose a round table for the eating space in the kitchen. As our first three children came along, the round table became the gathering point for our family at the evening meal. The children still remember that after the meal was prepared, the table set, and the grace spoken, Janet invariably breathed a sigh and said, "Let's all relax and enjoy this meal." At that round table we ate, snacked, debated, played games, read the Word, and prayed together. Seventeen years after the birth of our first child, the fourth came along. We learned then another advantage of the round table. To make room for Rob we simply scooted over, opened the space, and brought him in. Later, the children brought home boyfriends and girlfriends who became sons- and daughters-in-law. Again, we scooted over to make space for the new members of the family.

You'll understand, then, why I remember so well a family gathering on New Year's Eve after the older children were grown and making homes of their own. As we gathered one more time at the round table, we remembered how God had blessed us during the past year and prayed for His guidance in the year ahead. Our oldest son, Doug, had come home from his first year in graduate school. His prayer began with the words, "Thank You, Lord, for our round table."

Make Room at the Table

Picture a Jewish family celebrating one of their many feasts at a round table like ours. Mother says, "Let's relax and enjoy this meal."

Afterward, all listen as the father of the family tells the spiritual story behind the feast with its meaning in past history, its current significance, and its future hope. Now, visualize an Arab couple walking into the kitchen. With one look, the Jewish family members see them, scoot over, and invite them to join the celebration as full members of the family, even if it means giving up a portion of their food so that all might be served. Only grace can do that.

A dinner setting is also the way to understand what the apostle Paul means when he tells the Ephesians that the Jews and Gentiles are to be "sharers" (1) of God's promise; (2) in Christ; (3) through the gospel.

What's for Dinner?

The phrase "sharers of God's promise" is like asking, "What's for dinner?" and being given the menu. The substance of our hope is the promise that Paul expounded in detail in the third chapter of Galatians. As Abraham received the promise that his children would be the members of the family of God, he also received the word, "In thee . . . shall all the families of the earth be blessed" (Gen. 29:14, KJV). That same blessing comes to us through faith in Jesus Christ. We, too, are the children of Abraham, the children of God, and the children of promise. On that certainty Paul writes, "There is neither Jew nor Greek, slave nor free, male nor female, for you are all one in Christ Jesus" (Gal. 3:28).

We have wandered far from God's promise. Robert Bellah has written a book titled *The Broken Covenant,* in which he describes us as a people living in a land of broken promises ranging all the way from our oaths of office to our marriage vows.

Christians must keep their promises. Robertson McQuilkin, president of Columbia Bible College and Seminary, resigned from his position in order to care for his wife, Muriel, a victim of Alzheimer's disease. In his letter of resignation to the board he wrote, "Some years ago, when it became clear that my wife was experiencing some form of dementia, I knew immediately, and said both to the board and others that when the time came that she would need me full time, she would have me. That time has come."

Shortly thereafter, he spoke to the students in chapel, saying:

The decision was made, in a way, 42 years ago when I promised to care for Muriel "in sickness and in health . . . till death do us part." So, as a man of my word, integrity has something to do with it. But so does fairness. She has cared for me fully and sacrificially all these years; if I cared for her for the next 40 years I would not be out of debt. Duty, however, can be grim and stoic. But there is more: I love Muriel. She is a delight to me—her childlike dependence and confidence in me, her warm love, occasional flashes of that wit I used to relish so, her happy spirit and tough resilience in the face of her continual distressing frustration. *I don't have to care for her; I get to!*

What a witness to the grace of God in a land of broken promises! Even though Robertson McQuilkin is as human as any of us, he gives us a glimpse of the faithfulness of God's promise to us. This is what it means to be sharers in God's promise—we who deserve no place at His table are invited by faith to the feast at which all His promises become ours.

Who's the Host?

The second phrase answers the question, "Who's the host for dinner?" Paul says that we are partakers of God's promise "in Christ." Here again, we are encountering what is called "the scandal of particularity," which means that Christ and Christ alone is our only hope for salvation.

What is obvious truth to us is not obvious to others. In 1987 at the World Methodist Council in Nairobi, I spoke on the theme for the conference, "Christ Alone for Our Salvation." My biblical outline specified Christ as *the only Name, the only Word, and the only Hope* by which we are saved. I felt as if I were carrying coals to Newcastle at a conference of world Methodism, but soon learned otherwise. Many churches in our Methodist family do not hear this message from the pulpits. Many church leaders and theologians in the Wesleyan tradition do not believe that our salvation is in Christ alone. When the media picked up the story of the conference, my message was set against the executive secretary of the World Council of Churches who spoke later in the week. He called for an ecumenism that avoids the scandal of particularity in order to reconcile our Christian faith with other world religions. Although the World Methodist Council offers this kind of forum, its leadership remains committed to historic Wesleyanism in its stand for holiness of life and evangelism in the world.

Even closer home, James Davison Hunter surveyed Evangelical Christian college and seminary students, asking, "Is the only hope for heaven through personal faith in Jesus Christ, except for those who have never heard the gospel?" Only 66 percent of the college students and 68 percent of the seminary students answered, "Yes." On this question and others, Hunter found students far more tolerant in theology, vocation, morality, family, and politics than those in the immediate past generation. His conclusion is that the coming generation of Evangelicals is like Bunyan's Pilgrim, still on the path to the Celestial City but, after a long sojourn in the Labyrinth of Modernity, less certain, less confident, and more vulnerable than ever.

George Gallup in his book *The People's Religion* suggests that these same questions will rise in importance as the 20th century ends and the 21st century begins. World religions are no longer distant from us. Asian and Arab immigrants are doubling in our population, becoming our neighbors, and bringing their religion with them. Whether or not the next generation of Christians will hold the conviction that our promise and hope is in Christ alone is a troubling and challenging question for all who believe the gospel.

What's the Occasion?

With food on the table and the host in the honored seat, the question arises, "What's the occasion?" Paul tells us that as partakers of God's promise in Christ, we are celebrants of the Good News.

Pessimism continues to be one of the tones that Evangelical Christians are communicating to the world through print and protest. Browsing in a bookstore will show best-sellers in both fiction and nonfiction sending out vibrations of impending doom. Have we taken our cue from Henry Kissinger who once advised, "Always sound pessimistic. People will think that you are wise." If that is the strategy behind the sound of pessimism, no one will want to be part of the Christian family.

I have a friend who had given up on the preaching he heard in his local United Methodist church. Knowing that he is an avid reader, I recommended every book on John Wesley, grace, redemption, and sanctification that I could find. After finishing some of the books, he called to ask, "What is the difference between being a born-again Christian and an Evangelical Christian?" I told him about Emily Harris, coauthor with her husband of the best-seller *I'm O.K., You're O.K.* When asked by a reporter if she were a born-again Christian, she responded, "I refuse to answer that question. If I tell you that I am a born-again Christian, you'll assume that you know everything about me."

Being born again is an event, but being an Evangelical is a life, an attitude, a tone, and a spirit. So I explained to my friend that "evangelical" comes from the biblical word *evangel* and means that we bear the message of the good news that Jesus Christ has saved us from sin. Expanding on that definition, I drew upon his Methodist background to say that Wesleyans communicate the good news of the gospel through the celebration of grace freely received and grace freely given. Silence fell on the phone line as he reflected, "I buy that even though I never heard it preached in my church." It wasn't long before he returned to the family of faith through the Wesleyan message of grace.

George Gallup has predicted that America's faith will become less Protestant, less Western, more Catholic, more Mormon, and more unaffiliated. His forecast goes hand-in-hand with *Time* magazine's feature article "The Browning of America," which states, "In the lifetime of our babies, if current trends continue, White Americans of European ancestry will be a minority in the nation." If so, will we open our round tables, scoot over, and invite others into God's promise as given to us in Christ through the good news of the gospel? Paul left no room for excuses. He preached to the Ephesians that it was time for the Jews to scoot over and make room for us— outcasts and strangers. At the round table of promise the apostle saw Jews and Gentiles, slave and free, men and women. Now, it is time for us to scoot over and at the same table in the family of faith make room for Hispanics, Asians, Africans, Indians, and Arabs and others—we are all one in Christ Jesus according to the gospel.

Seeing the World on Our Knees

We cannot think about dinner with Christ without remembering His example of servanthood in an after-dinner setting. As part of a chapel series on various forms of worship, the students of Asbury Theological Seminary asked me to lead a foot washing ceremony. Never having participated in this kind of service, I felt intimidated and yet knew that Jesus had washed the feet of His disciples after the Last Supper. So, I agreed.

On the morning of the service, I addressed the chapel and led a short liturgy for foot washing while wearing full academic garb. Then, following the example of Christ, I stripped off the proud colors of my doctoral hood, the prerogatives of my presidential robe and medal, and the pious vestments of my clerical status. Taking a towel, I wrapped it around my waist, knelt to the floor, and poured water into a basin. Sliding the bowl ahead of me, I moved on my knees to wash the feet of people who represented the different races, roles, and status of our congregation. Slipping off a shoe at a time, I washed and dried

- a narrow, yellow-skinned foot that characterized an Asian ancestry
- a perspiring foot that betrayed discomfort in the public setting
- an alabaster foot so dainty that it snuggled neatly into the palm of my hand
- an outsized foot so big that it extended beyond the borders of the bowl

- a trembling foot that completely caught me by surprise, and
- a heavily veined foot that showed the sign of advancing age

In those feet, I saw the whole world come together. I knew all of these people face-to-face as their president, but until then I didn't know them hand-to-foot as their servant. I knelt before a microcosm of the whole world, its people, and their need—without regard to race, sex, age, or status, including the brilliant and the troubled, the old and the young, the clumsy and the dainty, the calm and the anxious, the secure and the fearful.

On my knees with a towel around my waist, I got a God's-eye view of our 21st-century world. As our Wesleyan forefathers found, diversity enriches the family of faith and gives us unprecedented opportunity as Wesleyans to demonstrate the beauty of being one in the Spirit. I also knew why Paul, after trying to explain the mystery and the miracle by which we become heirs together with the Jews, members together of one body, and sharers together in the promise of Jesus Christ, could only break out into spontaneous praise, "Now unto him that is able to do exceeding abundantly above all that we ask or think, according to the power that worketh in us, unto him be glory in the church by Christ Jesus throughout all ages, world without end. Amen" (Eph. 3:20-21, KJV).

6
Quickened Conscience

"Wesleyans are a people for whom there is no beauty of personal holiness without the conscience of social holiness."

WESLEYANS ARE A PEOPLE whose conscience has been fully awakened the Holy Spirit. Along with our conviction that holiness is both personal and social, we believe that a quickened conscience is honed on a double edge. One side is keen and quick to respond to God through the promptings of the Holy Spirit. We feel that sensitivity tugging at the depths of our soul when we sing the verse from Charles Wesley's hymn:

> *Quick as the apple of an eye,*
> *O God, my conscience make.*
> *Awake my soul, when sin is nigh,*
> *And keep it still awake.*

The other side of our Wesleyan conscience is just as keen and tender. With the mind of the Spirit and the heart of love, we are sensitized to the plaintive cry of the poor, the painful screams of injustice, and the resounding consequences of sin in our society.

From the very beginning of our history, moral conviction and social compassion have been distinguishing qualities of the Wesleyan character. Our moral convictions have caused us to speak out on unpopular issues, such as human slavery, and our social compassion has prompted us to act on behalf of the poor, the sick, and the unwanted before community agencies or governmental programs could respond.

Today, with the moral crisis escalating and becoming more and more complex, the double-edged Wesleyan conscience must be sharper than ever. It will go dull on either edge if we lose an intimate relationship with the Holy Spirit as our indwelling presence. When that happens, we begin to blink at sin that breaks the heart of God and to hide behind a thousand excuses over which He weeps. We also jump on bandwagons of popular causes that carry little risk and require no self-sacrifice.

Throughout human history, God's people have come to moments of moral crisis in which there is no place to hide. Their convictions and their compassion are put to a life-and-death test. One of those moments is recorded in the Old Testament when the destiny of the Jews fell directly upon the shoulders of Queen Esther. Under inspiration as well as desperation, her uncle Mordecai framed the crisis in the immortal words, "Yet who knows whether you have come to the kingdom for such a time as this?" (Esther 4:14, NKJV).

More than once, Wesleyans have had to ask and answer the same question. John Wesley had to respond in 18th-century England, and Francis Asbury had to answer in 19th-century America. Without falling into the trap of "manifest destiny" or assuming the arrogance of "triumphalism," they moved with confidence into the moral crisis of their era. From them, the Holiness Movement gained confidence for its mission in the latter half of the 19th and on into the 20th century. Under the legacy of earlier Methodism, Holiness leaders and people believed they were chosen "to spread scriptural holiness across the land, and reform the nation." As we learned in the closing decades of the 20th century, without this compelling vision for which we will live and die, our movement will stutter, if not stop.

All is not lost. Once again we are confronting a moral crisis of global proportions that will reverberate through the 21st century. Will Wesleyans step into the breach with the double edge of a quickened conscience and deepened compassion? Will we be compelled by the vision that scriptural holiness and social reform are inseparable? Will we be ready to live and die for that vision? By scanning our moral universe and seeing our moral crises, we will know why we must believe, experience, and practice scriptural holiness as the hope for spiritual awakening in our homeland and moral transformation around the globe.

I. Our Moral Universe

Like the "wash" of muted tones behind the details of a watercolor painting, only broad brush strokes can be used to portray the moral universe of our time. Most of the colors are grim. As far back as 1978, James Reston, *New York Times* columnist, told an Evangelical Congress on the Laity, "We are living in a moral pigsty." In that same period, Jacques Ellul, lawyer-theologian, saw our world possessed by "New Demons"; Robert Nisbet, social historian, feared that we were teetering on the brink of a "New Despotism"; Pitirim Sorokin, Harvard sociologist, diagnosed our age as a "Sensate Culture"; and Daniel Yankelovich described us living in an "upside down world" dominated by a cult of narcissism.

Even the alleged return to traditional values in the Reagan era did not quell the dire predictions of our moral condition. Robert Bellah, respected sociologist, in his book *Habits of the Heart* saw radical self-interest, not the common good, as the primary influence in shaping the emerging American character. Alan Bloom added another dimension to our dilemma by publishing *The Closing of the American Mind,* in which he pronounced moral bankruptcy on an academic community that had forsaken the values of absolute truth.

Our moral crisis came into focus in the 1990s with the election of Bill Clinton as president of the United States. To bolster the case for political conservatives, he brought with him moral baggage from his past that continued to plague his administration despite popularity at home and abroad. William Bennett, the converted Democrat and former secretary of education, took leadership in conservative ranks by publishing such books as *A Moral Compass, Our Sacred Honor,* and *The Death of Outrage.* Still, from a moral standpoint, the 20th century went out with a whimper and the 21st century inherited its crisis.

At the risk of reciting the obvious, I choose to describe the moral universe of our time by the up-and-down Chinese character that spells "crisis." On top is the symbol for "evident danger," but underneath is the graphic sign for "hidden opportunity." Both aspects, evident danger and hidden opportunity, hang suspended in the crisis of our time. To depict this dilemma, three images come into view: *a lifeboat, a waterhole, and an earthquake.*

Limited Lifeboats

A lifeboat symbolizes the ethical dilemma of life-and-death decisions. As long as there are enough lifeboats to go around, humans can cope with sinking ships. But as was depicted in the movie *Titanic,* ethical emergencies arise when there are more passengers than lifeboats. In this dilemma, choices must be made between those who will live and those who will die. Lifeboat ethics identify the moral crisis of our rights and responsibilities.

The Crisis of Life. Life-and-death decisions in medicine are the dramatic examples of moral choice. When I checked into the emergency room at the local hospital with chest pains, I was walked into a room with the sign "Triage." Unlike most patients, I knew immediately what it meant. During World War II, the number of wounded soldiers coming from the front lines overwhelmed the emergency units of medical staff and supplies. To deal with the problem, three sets (or a "triage") of emergency tents were set up. In the first group, wounded soldiers who would recover with or without medical treatment were placed. In the third group, they placed those who were so severely wounded that no amount of treatment would save their lives. In the second set of tents, then, were the soldiers who had a chance to live if treated immediately. A moral decision had to be made. With not enough medical supplies to go around, those who had a chance of recovery with treatment were attended first. Others lived or died on their own. In my case, the long period of waiting in the emergency room gave me hope that I was among those who would survive with or without treatment.

Biomedical ethics are even more dramatic. Science has sped ahead of our moral guidelines with such questions as, "Should the tissue of a naturally aborted fetus be used for medical experiments that might save human life?" "How do you counsel a young couple whose genetic background makes it highly probable that their child will be born defective?" "Should a Christian sign a living will in order to die with dignity?" and "Will Kevorkian ultimately win his case for medically assisted death?"

On the fringe of the future is a catalog of even more complex ethical dilemmas. Vance Packard, in his book *People Shapers,* has indexed these issues, such as genetic manipulation to select qualities and screen out defects in human reproduction, psychosurgery to modify human behavior, and cloning to preserve human identity. Although David Rorvik's controversial book *In His Image: The Cloning of a Man* was considered a commercial hoax until the ewe sheep Dolly was cloned, he will be remembered as the person who alerted us to the nightmarish question, "Does a cloned duplicate of the human being have a separate soul?"

The Crisis of Rights. Less dramatic than medical ethics, but just as critical to our moral future, is the question of individual rights. As with limited lifeboats, there are not enough rights to go around so that everyone can do as one wishes. Put another way, the rights of your elbow stop where my ribs begin.

For the sake of definition, three levels of individual rights can be identified. At the first level are *human rights,* defined in our democracy as the inalienable rights of life, liberty, and the pursuit of happiness. At home, we are learning the limits of these rights in such controversial questions as flag burning, television violence, gun control, and Internet gambling. Abroad, the equally controversial question is whether or not we can impose these human rights upon developing nations and totalitarian governments as a condition of trade and aid.

Upon the base of human rights is built *civil rights*—the guarantee of equal opportunity in the political, social, educational, and economic structure of our democracy with regard to the characteristics of birth—race, sex, age, and ethnic or national origin. After years of heated debate and legislative action, for instance, the regulations of affirmative action that were written in the 1960s to assure equal opportunity for racial minorities are under fire as failures. Such examples as school busing, minority hiring, and preferential school admissions are sufficient to remind us that the cause of civil rights is still a moral crisis in our midst.

Once our human and civil rights are promised or achieved, *personal rights* come into focus. Personal rights are defined as the rights of choice and conscience involving such matters as religion, politics, marriage, and morality, including sexual preference. Whether the question is a woman's right to choose an abortion, a cohabitating lesbian couple's right to receive the same health benefits as a married heterosexual couple, a Seventh-Day Adventist's right to refuse to work on Saturday, or a president's right to privacy in an adulterous affair, the issue of personal rights is fast becoming the new battleground for establishing ethical standards.

At stake in these controversies over human, civil, and personal rights is the moral center of our society. Whenever the ethical consensus in a society begins to erode, the pendulum swings wildly toward personal rights and moral chaos. Like the inhabitants of hell in C. S. Lewis's *The Great Divorce,* the sin of self-interest is the centrifugal force that causes individuals to flee outwardly and away from each other. As Robert Bellah has written in his sequel to *Habits of the Heart,* titled *The Common Good,* a radical self-interest shapes our institutions as it has already shaped our individual character. In a sobering summary, Bellah writes, "Our homes, schools and churches have become arenas of hostile self-interest rather than places where the common good is nurtured."

In the realistic terms of sinful human nature, only negotiated contracts can keep us from killing each other. Omens of the crisis are too close for comfort. Interpersonal relationships that were once established on good faith, sacred bonds, and total commitment—husband and wife, doctor and patient, teacher and student, employer and employee—are now held together by negotiated contracts and adversarial agreements. We should not be surprised that the courts are rapidly becoming the most powerful branch of government and we have become known as "litigious people," ready to sue at a moment's notice. When self-interest is reigning and the moral center is collapsing, the crisis of rights that began in a lifeboat ends up in a courtroom or in a show of violence.

Shrinking Waterholes

Another ethical emergency is visualized by the image of a shrinking waterhole. In the African game country, wild animals that are mortal enemies will organize a "drinking order" at a waterhole when there is plenty of water to go around. Drought can upset the established system. As the waterhole shrinks and the water supply diminishes, vicious killer instincts and even cannibalism appear among the animals. If the drought persists so that the waterhole shrinks to survival margins, a temporary truce is called. Weakened lions, antelope, wolves, and elephants come together to drink in peace because of a common, all-consuming thirst.

We are drinking at a shrinking waterhole of *physical resources*. Scarcity of resources, pollution of the environment, and density of population have already bared the fangs of our killer instincts. Persistent warnings go unheeded despite evidence of global warming, overpopulation, energy depletion, and food shortages around the world and evidence of blackouts, freeze-outs, flash floods, and drought at home. Whether or not we agree with the crusade of environmentalists, such as Albert Gore, we cannot deny that the devastation of El Niño has caused us to stop and think twice. Still, we follow the trail of a "cowboy economy" described by Kenneth Boulding as an attitude that consumes scarce resources on the range, leaves the waste at the campsite, and moves on to repeat the process at the next oasis.

Add the dilemma of *density* in our exploding urban populations. Years ago, biological research showed that deer mice, known as the best of community builders among small animals, could be turned into cannibals by increasing the density of their population beyond the available resources of space, water, and food. As a city dweller who fights gridlock, feels the anger of "road rage," and fears the possibility of a drive-by shooting, I see parallels between the deer mice and our urban population.

An ethical crisis confronts us. Will we in the Western world continue to grow industrially at the price of polluting the earth and using up our limited resources? Will we take a stance on the control of the world's population? Will we share the products of our wealth with the poor and wretched of the earth? Will we voluntarily conserve our limited resources or will compulsory control be required to curb our selfishness?

Prosperous Americans, and particularly we who are Christians, must face the ethical *dilemma of our affluence*. While our growth economy continues to be fed by our voracious consumer appetites, our core of moral values—based upon compassion and sacrifice—are being eaten away. Daniel Bell, in his book *The Cultural Contradictions of Capitalism,* sees us embracing a "hedonism which promises material ease and luxury, yet shies away from all of the historical implications which a 'voluptuary system' implies."

Closely related to our insatiable consumer appetite is the unspoken crisis between our *ethics of work and ethics of leisure.* In the Puritan tradition, discipline so guided our work that a dance around the Maypole represented a generous reward of our leisure. Now, the scale has tipped to the opposite extreme. Leisure time is increasing at the rate of 4 percent a year and television is absorbing 46 percent of that discretionary time. Before trying to resolve the global problems of industrial growth, environmental pollution, and the distribution of wealth, we need to clear the materialistic clutter in our personal lives and discipline the hedonistic impulses of our leisure time.

A shrinking waterhole of physical resources—whether time, space, money, or energy—provokes a crisis in values that can be summed up in the standoff between *freedom and control.* When the dilemmas of growth, distribution, and control of resources are balanced off against the chaotic demands of personal rights, the scenario of the future will have to include the possibility of what George Cabot Lodge called a "Totalitarian Lurch" away from our cherished freedoms and toward the centralized control of a modern-day Caesar.

Predictable Earthquakes

To complete this triad of images depicting our moral crisis, the rumble of a *predictable earthquake* comes to mind. Three quarters of the way through the 20th century, *Harper's* magazine published an article on our emerging moral crisis under the title "Goodbye, San Francisco." Millions of people live on the San Andreas Fault in the San Francisco Bay area. By and large, they are oblivious to the scientists' consensus that an earthquake of major proportions is only a matter of "when?" not "if?" In lay language, the author describes the plates of the earth grating against each other along the fault line.

As pressure builds when the plates grind, relief can come only when the surface of the earth erupts. Scientists know that the pulse of the earth beats an agitated, irregular tempo when earthquakes threaten. But, like the calm before the storm, the beat mysteriously returns to normal just before the earth erupts.

Predictable earthquakes remind us of our moral crisis in *authority*. Competing ideologies and conflicting systems of truth in our day are like the grinding plates of the earth. For years now, preachers have spotted that disjuncture and social scientists have surveyed it, but only the Doobie Brothers put it to music. As a complement to the *Harper's* article, "Goodbye, San Francisco," they came out with an album titled *Living on the Fault-line* with a cover that showed the needlepoint of the Transamerica building in San Francisco balancing on a narrow spit of sandy beach between a rocky bluff and the roaring ocean surf. After several frustrating attempts to tune my ears to the words behind the noise of the music, my teenage daughter deciphered lyrics that spoke of the uncertainty of the "stirrin'" in the earth and the inescapable nature of the awesome quake!

We know now what is stirring. Ideological worlds are in collision, and a moral earthquake of cataclysmic proportions is not a question of "if?" but "when?"

Even secular prophets have seen the eruption coming. Studs Terkel, the itinerant observer of common people, summed up his visits across America in the book *The Great Divide*. Although Terkel was a self-professed agnostic, he discovered a deep division in America along religious lines, which he felt had reached crisis proportions. On the religious right, he found the conservatives hunkered down behind the walls to protect the ethic of pro-life, the theology of biblical inerrancy, and the ecclesiology of independent churches. On the religious left, he observed another fortress mentality around the ethic of feminism, the theology of liberation, and the ecclesiology of ecumenical organic unity. Pressing further his analogy of the great divide, Terkel found both sides lobbing explosive missives at each other over the chasm, but leaving in the breach an ever-widening spiritual void to be filled by others.

Robert Wuthnow, Yale sociologist, added insight to the collision between ideological worlds with the publication of his book *Culture Wars*. With the question of revealed and absolute truth as the issue at stake, he discovered a deep division threatening the moral foundations of our national life. As strange as it may seem, he also discovered a new alliance among former enemies as conservative Jews, Roman Catholics, and Evangelical Christians bonded together in the belief that biblical revelation is the source of absolute Truth. *Time* magazine, in an article called "Mainline Blues," surveyed the same spiritual void between ideological worlds in the questions that people are asking:

Who am I before God?

How can I be saved from sin?

How can I face my own death?

If Christians fail to answer these questions, the spiritual void between left and right becomes fair ground for the heresies of half-truth and the human sophistries, such as the New Age movement. Paul warned us against these heresies in his Letter to the Colossians when he wrote, "See to it that no one takes you captive through hollow and deceptive philosophy, which depends upon human tradition and the basic principles of the world rather than on Christ" (2:8).

Adding their insight to inspired truth, social researchers point out that young, affluent, educated, and professional people are prime prospects for these cults. New Age literature, for instance, became a major factor in the growth of the publishing industry in the last two decades of the 20th century. While our crisis is moral, our conflict is spiritual.

II. OUR MORAL RESPONSE

Scanning the moral crisis of our time leaves one feeling like the father who started out on a cross-country trip with four kids in a Volkswagen Beetle. After 100 miles of traveling with them, he was convinced of original sin. Another hundred miles and he had no doubt about total depravity!

Robert Heilbroner came to a similar conclusion when he wrote *An Inquiry into the Human Prospect.* At one time, he writes, Prometheus, the Grecian god who carried fire to the top of the mountain as a symbol of human achievement, represented the idealistic ambitions of our society. Now, Heilbroner says that Atlas has taken center stage, bearing the weight of the world in his hands, struggling to stay alive, and hoping to "rescue the future from the angry condemnation of the present."

Perhaps James Reston spoke for us all when he denounced our society as a "moral pigsty" and then asked his born-again audience, "What is the connector between your personal morality and our public morality?" A world awaits the evidence that spiritual rebirth will lead to social renewal in our generation. Put another way, the born-again movement of the 1970s needs the touch of personal and practical holiness to be a transforming force in the public arena.

Admittedly, the distinction between personal and practical holiness is artificial. I use the term "personal holiness" to define the dynamic experience of the cleansing and empowering work of the Holy Spirit in the human heart. But then, when we encounter the moral crisis of the world in which we live, the power of personal holiness must be translated into the ethics of practical holiness. Early Methodists used the term "practical holiness" to describe the daily dimensions of perfect love. For them, entire sanctification was not just doctrinal theory but an experience hammered out in response to the spiritual need and moral crisis of 18th-century England. Using Bernard Semmel's book *The Methodist Revolution* as a source, his understanding of practical holiness is worthy of review.

The Character of Practical Holiness

Practical holiness begins with the Christian discipline of our character. In 1786, at the age of 83, John Wesley wrote from the depths of his soul, "I am not afraid that the people called Methodist should ever cease to exist either in Europe or America. But I am afraid, lest they should only exist as a dead sect, having the form of religion without power. And this is undoubtedly the case, unless they hold fast the doctrine, spirit and discipline with which they first set out."

We often speak of the Wesleyan quadrilateral for theological balance—revelation, reason, tradition, and experience. In Wesley's words, we also find the Methodist triangle for spiritual renewal—doctrine, spirit, and discipline.

- *To preach and teach Wesleyan doctrine* based upon biblical truth
- *To experience the infilling of the Holy Spirit* even if it means being charged with "enthusiasm"
- *To follow the discipline of holy living,* which separates us from sin and sensitizes us to human need

For such a time as this! Without falling into the rationalistic trap of proof-texting the truth or forcing the Word of God to fit our political agenda, we must preach and teach biblical, Wesleyan doctrine with the confidence and clarity of a catechism for the rising generation.

Howard Snyder, one of our foremost Wesleyan historians, published the book *Signs of the Spirit*. It is a historical study of spiritual renewal movements, including the Methodist Revolution of the 18th century. After sorting through the common elements in the renewal movements, Synder comes to the conclusion that the starting point in every case is renewal though the rediscovery of the gospel. The rediscovery may be personal, as with John Wesley's heartwarming experience at Aldersgate, or conceptual, as with Count Von Zinzendorf's development of Hernhutt as a refuge for the poor. In either case, the gospel took on new meaning and energized a spiritual revolution.

What do we need to rediscover in the gospel for the moral crisis of our time? The answer comes from every sector of religion today, whether theological left or right, church or sect, Wesleyan or Reformed, Protestant or Catholic, Evangelical or Mainline. In common, *we thirst for holiness.* Snyder notes this thirst as another motive force for spiritual renewal. "Holiness" is a word that is being redeemed today, and for Wesleyans it should be the word for which there is no apology. Francis Asbury joined with Wesley in common prayer when he wrote in his journal in 1779, "My soul is waiting on the Lord for full Christian perfection. I poured out my soul to the Lord for this, and for my brethren in all parts of the world, that the power of religion may continue with us, as a people. I tremble to think of the cloud of the divine presence departing from us; if this should be, I hope not to live to see it."

As an observer of the groundswell for spirituality coming across the religious landscape, I cannot help but note that Reform theologians tend to *legalize* holiness, Roman Catholics *sacramentalize* it, and Charismatics *emotionalize* it. Of course, all of these elements enter into Wesleyan spirituality, but not as isolated or overemphasized parts. Missing is the Wesleyan dynamic of "perfect love," which brings obedience, sacrament, and emotion into one, integrated experience when the Spirit of God moves upon our souls. Without that dynamic and that balance, the discipline will die, the formation will fail, and the tongues will cease. Responsibility for the experiential balance of practical holiness or "faith working through love," rests with us.

John Wesley saw the need for defining practical holiness as the moral character of a Spirit-filled person. Wesley penned *The Character of a Methodist* when he was asked, "What are the distinguishing marks of a Methodist?" He wrote:

> By salvation, a Methodist means holiness of heart and life. . . . A Methodist is a person who has the love of God in his heart . . . cares about his neighbor as much as himself . . .

> God has cleaned the Methodist's heart, washing away all urge for revenge . . . envy . . . wrath . . . harm . . . unkind inclination . . . evil lust and desire . . . pride . . . haughtiness. He cannot devote himself to selfish indulgence, preoccupied with making money . . . The Christian thinks, speaks and lives according to the pattern of Jesus. I ask no further questions. Do you love God? This is enough. I give you the right hand of fellowship.

Are these distinguishing marks of a Methodist still applicable for us?

Not without significance, when Richard Quebedeaux wrote his book *The New Evangelicals,* he used Wesley's words to describe "The New Wesleyans" of our day. To be part of that company, however, we need to recapture the spiritual discipline behind the Christian character.

There is a strong and commendable emphasis upon the Body of Christ as a loving, caring community. Missing is what Dean Kelley in his book *Why Conservative Churches Are Growing* has called "the power of the gate." The gate swings wide open when converts are taken into fellowship and agree to be part of the discipline of holy living. Within the gate, mature Christians model out the qualities of the Spirit-filled life and monitor the growth of new believers. If, however, individuals turn from the faith, reject the discipline, the gate must swing out in exit, but only after patience of truth in love and the provision to start again. As in Wesley's time, specific temptations and sins must be addressed. His converts were saved from profanity, drunkenness, and immorality. Their newfound industry as Christian converts created problems of handling money and time. Thus, the discipline of stewardship became evidence of practical holiness before the world.

Times have not changed. The moral crisis of resources again calls for the discipline of stewardship for the new money and new leisure that we enjoy. Without a sound biblical ethic, we tend to swing between extremes. At one extreme is the call for a nostalgic return to a simple lifestyle; at the other is the heady arrogance of a prosperity gospel. All of us need to reread William Law's *A Serious Call to a Devout and Holy Life,* in which he calls for the "devotion of the common life"—or the discipline of perfection in the business of life.

The Compassion of Holiness

Practical holiness continues with the moral motivation to preach the gospel to the socially poor and spiritually lost. Jesus gives us our example. In the glory of the baptism, the Spirit of God descended upon Him in the form of a dove, and God sealed His indwelling presence with the verbal witness that Jesus was His beloved Son in whom He was well-pleased. The same Spirit led into the wilderness and guided Him through Satan's temptation. In His first public utterance, Jesus testified to the experience of personal holiness when He said, "The Spirit of the Lord is upon me" (Luke 4:18a, KJV). Without waiting a moment to bask in the glory of that experience, He proceeds to the vocation of practical holiness: "He hath anointed me to preach the gospel to the poor; he hath sent me to heal the brokenhearted, to preach deliverance to the captives, and recovering of sight to the blind, to set at liberty them that are bruised, to preach the acceptable year of the Lord" (Luke 4:18b-19, KJV).

John Wesley, the Oxford don, Anglican churchman, and loyalist to the king, was led along the same path under the direction of the Holy Spirit. On March 31, 1739, he records in his journal, "In the evening I reached Bristol and met Mr. Whitefield there. I could scarcely reconcile myself at first to the strange way of preaching in the fields . . . I had been all my life so very tenacious of every point relating to decency and order that I should have thought the saving of souls almost a sin if it had not been done in church."

The next day was Sunday. In church, he expounded on the Sermon on the Mount and was awakened to the fact that this was "one pretty remarkable precedent for field-preaching" (Wesley's Journal, April 1, 1739). Monday, the next day, made history. Wesley now writes in his journal, "At four in the afternoon, I submitted to be more vile and proclaimed in the highways the glad tidings of salvation. The scripture on which I spoke was this: 'The Spirit of the Lord is upon me, because He has anointed me to preach the gospel to the poor; He hath sent me to heal the broken-hearted, to preach deliverance to the captives, and recovering of sight to the blind, to set at liberty them that are bruised, to proclaim the acceptable Year of the Lord.'"

Who are the broken, bound, blind, and bruised among us today? In the World News section of every daily newspaper, we read about the wretched of the earth. In addition to the hundreds of millions who are starving from the lack of food, there are 70 million others who are diseased and dying simply because they lack clean water. Another 30 million or more go blind because they lack a touch of ointment on their eyes. My heart is wrenched with compassion, and I am ready to give up everything for a "clean water" and "clean eye" crusade as my ministry to the needy of the world.

But then the Spirit of God checks me as I read the Local News section of the same paper. The Bureau of Census reports a doubling of the number of unmarried men and women living together, almost a doubling of divorces in the last two decades, the multiplication of abused and abandoned children who are the "new poor" among us, and the skyrocketing statistics of abuse and addiction. I have to think again about the broken, bound, blind, and bruised among us. We need practical holiness to change our attitudes and our direction. The testimony, "The Spirit of the Lord is upon me, because he hath anointed me," must advance to the task of healing, delivering, recovering, and freeing the broken, blind, bound, and bruised in our time and down our street.

The Conviction of Practical Holiness

As our third response to moral crisis, practical holiness holds forth a moral standard for the renewal of the society. In the First Epistle of John we read, "We are of God: he that knoweth God heareth us; he that is not of God heareth not us. Hereby know we the spirit of truth, and the spirit of error" (4:6, KJV).

Through the mind of the Holy Spirit, we get the convictions by which we discern truth from error. In Wesley's time, the conviction of perfect love stood for justice against human slavery. As a logical consequence of the Arminian doctrine of unlimited atonement, Wesley preached the natural rights of all men for social as well as spiritual freedom. Although the connection may not be direct, historians see the spiritual freedom of the Great Awakening of the mid-1700s in colonial America as fuel for the colonist's drive for political freedom from the tyranny of England.

If there is an issue testing Christian conscience today, it is still the question of social justice. In one way or another, every moral crisis touches on this issue. Why is it that our forefathers were known as champions of justice while we shy away from its implications?

A classic case is the Jewish Holocaust during World War II. As we know now, except for a handful of Lutheran pastors in Nazi Germany, Christian leaders of the world, including the pope, failed to lead the cry of moral outrage on behalf of the Jews. Martin Niemöller, one of those Lutheran pastors, was imprisoned in a concentration camp where 76,000 Jews died. When released, he was asked, "How did the world let this happen?" Niemöller answered, "In Germany, the Nazis first came for the Communists, and I didn't speak up because I wasn't a Communist. Then they came for the Jews, and I didn't speak up because I wasn't a Jew. Then they came for the trade unionists, and I didn't speak up because I wasn't a trade unionist. Then they came for the Catholics, and I didn't speak up because I was a Protestant. Then they came for me, and by that time there was no one left to speak for me."

When the Spirit of God calls us to the moral standard of Christian conviction, it is always at a risk. Our recent history does not commend us as risk-takers for the cause of social justice. In fact, our record as advocates for racial, economic, and political justice at home and abroad aligns us with the silent majority of which Niemöller spoke. When we do take our positions, they are politically predictable, publicly safe, or long past due.

In the early 1990s, I served as secretary of the National Religious Partnership on the environment as an Evangelical Christian representative. Leadership for the partnership came from Albert Gore before he was elected as vice president of the United States and Carl Sagan, our best-known physical scientist and avowed atheist. Other members of the partnership were the national leaders of Roman Catholic, Jewish, and Protestant traditions. I knew that accepting the position would mean criticism from within the Evangelical community because we have been woefully silent on the subject of the environment. My reading of Scripture, however, told me that our biblical stewardship as outlined in the Genesis account of creation mandated a responsibility for the environment as one of God's good but endangered gifts. Biblical conviction took me into the most diverse theological company I had ever known and led to me to accept the position as secretary in order to serve as an Evangelical voice in shaping the policies and pronouncements of the partnership.

In our meetings, I quickly learned that most of the members had an Evangelical passion for saving the environment. Albert Gore had taken that position in his book *Earth in the Balance: Ecology and the Human Spirit,* and Jewish leaders in America equated the crusade with the salvation of humankind. Carl Sagan, of course, just smiled and let the meter run in his favor. As might be expected, then, when the mission statement of the partnership was framed, a biblical foundation was missing. This gave me my chance to speak and remind the group that the source of our mandate did not come from scientific discovery or human survival but from the Genesis account of creation in which God pronounced His work as "Very good" and gave us responsibility to "tame and tend" the garden of His making. Whether or not the other members understood or accepted what I proposed, a sentence on biblical stewardship was inserted that could be used as a reminder of our spiritual responsibility time and time again.

Reflecting upon that experience, I am convinced that Wesleyan-Holiness leaders must seek out the opportunities of risk in which they can be a part of shaping the conscience of the country on the issues of justice. A half century ago, Carl F. H. Henry in *Aspects of Christian Social Ethics* gave us a model for Evangelical social action that needs to be resurrected. He saw four strategies for Christian involvement in society:

1. *Regeneration*—redeeming individuals who morally and spiritually influence their culture.
2. *Education*—teaching individuals the moral and spiritual implications of social issues.

3. *Legislation*—lobbying for laws that uphold a moral foundation and regulate moral behavior.
4. *Revolution*—seeking to overturn an evil regime by civil disobedience and, if necessary, by physical force.

Using this model, three principles guide us in Evangelical Christian social action. *First, regeneration is the primary responsibility of the Church and Christians in society.* "Let the Church be the Church" is our clarion call. *Second, the Church has a secondary responsibility for educating society on moral and spiritual issues according to the biblical standard.* Education cannot be a substitute for regeneration. *Third, the Church has a tertiary responsibility for legislative action because of the danger of politicizing our primary mission of regeneration.* Individual Christian action based upon educational understanding and spiritual discernment is absolutely essential for us as citizens of the society. *Fourth, revolution must be the last resort for Evangelical Christians in social action.* Civil disobedience should be exercised only when the democratic means (i.e., legislation or judicial decision) fail so that Christians must decide whether to obey God or man. Physical force can only be justified when the existing regime takes over the regeneration function of the Church and claims to be the source of human salvation.

While Henry's model does not give easy answers to the issues of our current moral crisis, it is one of our best guides for opening the discussion and applying the principles for us, both as individual Christians and as the institutional Church. A quick reading of the contemporary scene, for instance, would call the Church back to its priority for regeneration, strengthen our educational system for biblical understanding, screen our lobbying for legislative issues that detract from our primary mission, and question any movement that short-circuits the democratic process to mount illegal protests or justify physical violence. Wesleyans, in particular, will find opportunity to demonstrate practical holiness through these principles.

The Confidence of Practical Holiness

Practical holiness has at least one other contribution to make to our moral crisis. Often neglected is the *confidence* of the Spirit-filled life. As a maverick in the Wesleyan-Holiness community, I have never been willing to equate holiness with low self-esteem. After reading the history of our Wesleyan forefathers, such as John Wesley and Francis Asbury, and the biographies of our Holiness leaders, I see humility and confidence commingled as further evidence of the Spirit-filled life.

Many are tempted to panic in the midst of moral crisis or become pessimistic about the future. Oftentimes, the crisis is turned into proof that evil is in control and the Second Coming is imminent. I nursed these fears as a teenage Christian until I was introduced in high school to the poem by John Greenleaf Whittier titled "Abraham Davenport." Whittier wrote the poem in the aftermath of the famous "Day of Darkness" that engulfed New England on May 19, 1780.

When a "horror of great darkness" fell over the land, men prayed and women wept, listening for the "doom-blast of the trumpet" and looking for the "dreadful face of Christ." In the old State House of Connecticut, the lawgivers trembled and said, "It is the Lord's Great Day! Let us adjourn." But then they turned to Abraham Davenport, who cleaved the intolerable hush with a steady voice:

> This may well be
> The Day of Judgment for which the world awaits;
> But be it so or not, I only know
> My present duty, and my Lord's command
> To occupy till He come. So at the post
> Where He hath set me in His providence,
> I choose, for one, to meet Him face to face—
> No faithless servant frightened from my task,
> But ready when the Lord of Harvest calls;
> And therefore, with all reverence, I would say,
> Let God do His work, we will see to ours,
> Bring in the candles.

Then, straight to the issue and with a dry natural sense of humor, Abraham Davenport debated an amendment to an act regulating shad and alewife fisheries:

> And there he stands in memory to this day,
> Erect, self-poised, a rugged face, half seen
> Against the background of unnatural dark,
> A witness to the ages as they pass,
> That simple duty hath no place for fear.

How much that sounds like Peter's call to practical holiness when he wrote, "But sanctify the Lord God in your hearts: and be ready always to give an answer to every man that asketh you a reason of the hope that is in you with meekness and fear" (1 Pet. 3:15, KJV).

Wesleyans are a people who do not panic under moral crisis. Rather, with an understanding of practical holiness, we go about our business of doing God's will in our daily routine—already ready for His coming but never paralyzed by panic. Even with unnatural darkness above and trembling fear, we can say with confidence, "Bring in the candles!"

7 Global Parish

"Wesleyans are a people who are ready to speak the gospel of grace and offer the service of love to all people, in all places, at any time."

WESLEYANS ARE A WORLDLY PEOPLE. Not in the traditional sense of the word but in the scope of their vision for the lost. When John Wesley dared to cross parish boundaries in order to preach in fields and marketplaces, the Anglican hierarchy tried to stop him. In bold response, Wesley invoked the authority of the Great Commission and announced, "I look upon all the world as my parish."

Our world has been turned upside down since Wesley's day. We are fast becoming citizens of a "global village" connected by instant communication. At the same time, we are becoming more diverse in racial, ethnic, social, and religious origins. Jesus' words at the final Judgment (Matt. 25) come to mind when He speaks about our responsibility for persons whom we do not know, like, or trust. Our world parish in the 21st century will not be a melting pot of people blending into white, Western, Christian, and Anglo-Saxon sameness, but a salad bowl in which racial, ethnic, sexual, social, and religious differences remain intact except for the dressing of our common humanity, which makes them palatable.

Wesleyans who are true to Christ's commission and Wesley's world vision will not shy away from our parish of tomorrow. Out of our history, we bring resources to the changing scene that are enhanced by time and change. *First, we inherit Wesley's willingness to become "vile" in order to preach the gospel of "deliverance, recovery,*

and liberty" to the poor. As he took to the fields and the marketplace, we must venture to those places in our world where human
need and spiritual opportunity converge. *Second, we are heirs of
Wesley's ability to create a network of ministry for reaching all people.* As Wesley rode a circuit around England on horseback; we
must ride a circuit around the world by media. From its beginning,
the Wesleyan movement has been "media friendly," whether in the
publication of Wesley's tracts or in the pioneer production of religious radio broadcasts. We must reclaim the concept of the circuit in
the electronic age in order to embrace our world. *Third, as Wesleyans we have received the pattern of our founder's organizational
genius for nurturing our converts into spiritual maturity.* Its effectiveness for developing discipleship and leadership has never been
questioned, and its model keeps reappearing in growing churches
and movements. We must rediscover that pattern, and especially the
motive that prompted it and the discipline that perpetuated it.
*Fourth, from our heritage, we have the legacy of Wesley's con-
science for social justice.* In the 21st century issues of social justice
on a global scale will continue to be as prickly as a bramble bush.
Yet, under the guidance of the Holy Spirit, John Wesley walked with
wisdom through thickets no less thorny. By his example, he has
much to teach us. *Fifth, and perhaps most of all, we bring his passion to win the lost and his compassion to serve the poor.* As Wesleyans demonstrate their passion for One and their compassion for
all, they will cross all boundaries with the message of grace and the
motive of love. Debates over the definition of holiness will become
moot as once again Wesleyans demonstrate the meaning of "faith
working through love."

With these resources for ministry in the 21st century, we can
claim with confidence, "The world is our parish." How do we, as
Wesleyans, become the people who are ready to preach the gospel
and serve the poor in all places, at any time?

I. COMPELLED BY CONVICTION

Anyone with the slightest sense of adventure will be inspired by
the vision of a world parish. To make the vision reality, however, is a
different matter. Two natural tendencies take over. One is to settle
down in the comfort level of our success at the local level. The other
tendency is to rework old territory rather than stretching out to new
and uncharted areas.

Our biblical precedent for a world parish counters both of these
natural tendencies. In the example of Jesus Christ and the apostle

Paul, we see the only motivation that makes sure that our vision of a world parish becomes a reality. By example, they show us what it means to be compelled by conviction.

The Momentum of Conviction

Jesus opened His public ministry in Capernaum with a busy day of preaching with authority, casting out unclean spirits, healing the sick, and shutting the mouths of demons. Like wildfire, His fame spread throughout Galilee and its surrounding regions. While anticipating a night of rest and prayer, Jesus is interrupted by Simon and the other disciples who announce to Him, "Everyone is looking for you!" (Mark 1:37). Weighing the implications of such popularity, Jesus responds with resolution, *"Let us move on* to the country towns in the neighbourhood; I have to proclaim my message there also; that is what I came out to do" (v. 38, NEB, emphasis added). Rejecting the temptation to settle down in the comfort of local popularity, Jesus gives us the incentive to "move on," not only from town to town but also from nation to nation and from continent to continent until the whole world is embraced.

The Risk of Conviction

Paul the apostle in his letter to the Romans complements the vision of Jesus when he writes, "It is my ambition to bring the Gospel to places *where the very name of Christ has not been heard,* for I do not want to build on another man's foundation; but, as Scripture says, 'They who had no news of him see, and they who never heard of him shall understand.' That is why I have been prevented all this time from coming to you" (Rom. 15:20-22, NEB, emphasis added). He might have been content to build upon his popularity among the seven churches of Asia Minor and to rework these territories with the assurance of acceptance and success. Certainly, Paul yearned to minister to the beleaguered Christians in Rome, the very center of pagan opposition. But the vision of God's redemptive plan for a lost world as seen through the eyes of the prophet Isaiah spurred him on. Without the advantage of market research, but with the mind of the Holy Spirit, Paul moved on under the singular compulsion "to bring the Gospel to places where the very name of Christ has not been heard" (NEB). There is no other path to the whole world. We must "move on" from our places of security and "move forward" into new and uncharted fields with the name of Christ.

The Boldness of Conviction

Centuries after Jesus and Paul, John Wesley also has to make a decision. In his journal he writes, "God in scripture commands me, according to my power, to instruct the ignorant, reform the wicked, confirm the virtuous. Man forbids me to this another's parish. That is, in effect, to do it at all, seeing that I have no parish of my own, nor probably, never shall. Whom then shall I hear, God or man?"

Responding to his own question, Wesley declares, "I look upon all the world as my parish; thus far I mean, that, in whatever part of it I am, I judge it meet, right and my bounden duty to declare unto all that are willing to hear, the glad tidings of salvation."

The Discipline of Conviction

Move forward two more centuries into the early 1970s. I invited Billy Graham to be our commencement speaker at Seattle Pacific University. Courteously, but without pretense or apology, Billy explained that each year he received more than 15,000 invitations to speak across the world. A majority of the invitations come from Christian organizations. Billy said, "I could spend all of my time speaking to groups who would applaud every word, but God has given me opportunities to preach where the name of Christ has not been heard. I would love to be with you, but I can't come."

The next week on public radio, I heard Dr. Graham addressing the National Press Club, answering their pointed questions without compromising the gospel. Afterward, I wrote him a note saying, "Now I understand why you turned me down. I want to learn the same lesson."

The Claims of Conviction

From a human standpoint, any of these claims seem presumptuous:

- Jesus Christ saying, "Let us move on."
- The apostle Paul saying, "I will not preach where others have preached" (paraphrased).
- John Wesley saying, "I look upon all the world as my parish."
- Billy Graham saying, "I cannot come."

After all, it takes an *air of audacity* to claim that you have a special calling to the whole world; it takes an *edge of arrogance* to assume that you have something special to say to that world; and it takes a *dose of ambition* to continue stretching out into uncharted territory where the very name of Christ has not been heard or understood.

II. COMMISSIONED BY GRACE

Paul, in his letter to the Romans, addresses each of these hazards as he expands upon his vision for the whole world. *First, he tells us that he is commissioned by grace to preach in a world parish.* Candidly, he confesses that he is writing to the Gentile Christians at Rome with a boldness bordering on audacity. Yet, he is equally quick to deny that his words are based on an attitude of superior goodness or superior knowledge. In fact, he compliments the Romans on the moral and intellectual maturity that makes them quite capable of teaching each other. Thus, his only purpose in speaking so boldly to them is to refresh their memory, and his only credential for writing so frankly to them is his commission from God. All of our being vibrates as we hear Paul testify, "I have written you quite boldly on some points, as if to remind you of them again, because of the grace God gave me to be a minister of Christ Jesus to the Gentiles" (Rom. 15:16).

Grace makes all of the difference in our claims to witness in a world parish. In ourselves we find no superior goodness or superior knowledge. We acknowledge that our own righteousness is as filthy rags and our own knowledge is like a clanging cymbal. With Paul, our only claim to offer Christ to others is the gift of grace that God has given us. As he had the commission of grace to preach to the Gentiles, we are commissioned by grace to make the world our parish.

The Intercession of Grace

John Stott, in his book *Between Two Worlds,* writes primarily for preachers, but his words apply for every witness of the gospel. Stott says, "He who proclaims the Gospel must be embraced by the Gospel." Going on, he quotes Charles Spurgeon who spoke with spice, "A graceless pastor is a blind man elected to be a professor of optics . . . while he himself is absolutely in the dark! He is a dumb man elevated to the chair of music; a deaf man fluent upon symphonies and harmonies! He is a mole professing to educate eaglets; a limpet elected to preside over angels."

In contrast to this unforgettable description of the graceless pastor, Stott remembers D. L. Moody, of whom a liberal critic confessed, "He has a right to preach the Gospel because he never speaks of a lost soul without a tear in his eye."

Paul also has a tear in his eye. He writes, "My priestly service is the preaching of the gospel of God" (Rom. 15:16, NEB). Preachers, like all of us, want to be prophets trumpeting a clear, pure note of truth, wielding a two-edged sword, and piercing the darkness with the laser light of the gospel. But where grace is involved, whether clergy or laity, we are commissioned to be priests—intercessors who weep and pray for those to whom the gospel is given.

The Sacrifice of Grace

Grace puts its own check on any arrogance about the results of our witness. Each of us would like to display people as trophies of our witness in the world. Paul is not so presumptuous. He sees his priestly responsibility to be offering up the Gentiles before God as an "acceptable sacrifice" (Phil. 4:18). His effectiveness is then sealed by the work of the Holy Spirit as people are redeemed and their witness of grace becomes the sweet smelling savor of the sacrifice consumed.

I learned about the priestly role of preaching the hard way. For years I beat myself unmercifully for hours and days after I spoke in the college chapel as I remembered the things I said and didn't say. One day a former student met me on the street and told me how his life had been changed by a sermon that I felt was the worst I had ever preached. The Holy Spirit broke through with the truth that after thorough preparation and faithful presentation, I must leave every sermon on the altar as a sacrifice for Him to use as He wills. Paul wrote what I learned. Through the eyes of grace received, he envisions a priestly role in offering Christ to the whole Gentile world and laying that world on the altar of God as an acceptable sacrifice for the Holy Spirit to consecrate and consume.

John Wesley also saw his world parish through the eyes of grace. Notably, he did not see a kingdom to be ruled or a land to be conquered. We can be sure that he would reject any contemporary movements of militant crusaders, arrogant reformers, or violent activists who claim the name of Christ. Along with Paul, Wesley sees a world parish in which he is a priest interceding for the lost with a tear in his eye, sacrificing himself for the needs of others, and letting the Holy Spirit determine the results. Until every Wesleyan, clergy or laity, young or old, great or small, sees himself or herself as a priest offering the sacrifice of grace, the vision of a global parish is a fleeting fantasy.

III. AUTHORIZED BY EXPERIENCE

To assume that the world is our parish might still smack of arrogance. Paul confronts that question as forcefully as he does the issue of his audacity by telling us that *he is authorized by experience to take the gospel to the Gentiles.* Straight out, he says, "I have ground for pride in the service of God" (Rom. 15:17, NEB). No apology is made for the use of the word "pride," which can also be translated "glory" or "boasting" in the service of God.

The Credentials of Character

Taken from the context, we are repelled by the thought of anyone who dares to admit a feeling of pride, a claim to glory, or a willingness to boast in the service of God. But just as grace puts Paul's boldness for preaching into focus, his experience in Jesus Christ puts his pride into perspective. He writes, "For I will not dare to speak of any of those things which Christ has not accomplished through me" (v. 18, NKJV). In paraphrase, Paul is saying that he will not preach above or beyond his experience.

What a threat to our witness! If we followed Paul's principle, many of us would have little say about the gospel. John Wesley was told to preach faith *until* he had it, but Paul would not preach faith *unless* he had it. Although the disciplined quality of Wesley's personal life limited the risk of contradiction between his preaching and his practice, Paul's principle is the one we should follow. Too many witnesses to the gospel, both clergy and laity, assume that we can separate speaking biblical truth from the way we live. It is like dividing the executive performance of a president from his character. Christians who are quick to call for consistency in our leadership must also be accountable for the consistency of their witness. Charles Spurgeon once described a man who was a good preacher, but a bad Christian, this way, "He preached so well and lived so badly, that when he was in the pulpit everyone said that he ought never to come out again, and when he was out of it they all declared that he ought never to enter it again" (John Stott, *Between Two Worlds*).

To illustrate this truth, the story is told about a British preacher who got on a local bus, needed change to pay his fare, and when seated, discovered that the driver had given him the wrong change. Because the error was in his favor, he debated whether or not to give it back to the driver. After all, he thought, I have often been shortchanged. Finally, when he arrived at his stop, he told the driver, "You made a mistake and gave me the wrong change." The driver answered, "It was no mistake. I heard your sermon on Sunday morning, and I wanted to find out if you really mean what you say." Each of us has had a similar experience. When we take the name "Christian," "Wesleyan," or "Evangelical," we invite the scrutiny of those who expect us to live up to our name.

The Credentials of Compassion

In quick succession, then, Paul adds "the force of miraculous signs and the power of the Holy Spirit" (Rom. 15:19, NEB) to his authority. If there is pride, glory, or boasting in our vision of a world parish, it is not our own. At best, we are instruments made new in Christ and tuned to the work of His Spirit so that by word, deed, and miraculous signs, Christ and Christ alone is glorified.

The end result is what Henri Nouwen calls the "authority of compassion." Only the person who is forgiven can communicate forgiveness. Only the person who is filled with the Spirit can communicate the Spirit-filled life. Without denying the personal gifts, professional skills, and leadership techniques that are needed to enhance our witness, Nouwen, in *The Wounded Healer,* says, "If priests and ministers of tomorrow think that more skilled training is the solution for the problem of Christian leadership for the future generation, they may end up being more frustrated and disappointed than the leaders of today. More training and structure are just as necessary as more bread for the hungry. But just as bread given without love can bring war instead of peace, professionalism without compassion will turn forgiveness into a gimmick, and the kingdom of God will come in a blindfold."

Wesleyans have much to learn from the principles that Paul developed to back up his vision for the world. With him we must say, "I will venture to speak of those things alone in which I have been Christ's instrument to bring the Gentiles into his allegiance, by word and deed, by the force of miraculous signs and by the power of the Holy Spirit" (Rom. 15:18-19, NEB). As priests in a world parish, the authority of experience is the key to our effectiveness.

IV. DISCIPLINED BY NEED

Made bold by the commission of grace and made proud by the glory of Christ, Paul announces his plan for reaching the world: "It is my ambition to bring the Gospel to places where the very name of Christ has not been heard" (Rom. 15:20, NEB).

In response to critics who may question his ambition, the apostle is saying that his drive is disciplined by need to preach to the Gentiles.

Among the hundreds of books that have been written on leadership during the past two decades, *Leadership: Strategies for Taking Charge* by Warren Bennis and Bert Nanus stands out. The authors interviewed 90 top leaders to determine whether they had characteristics in common. Among their findings is the fact that leaders are risk-takers. At the risk of failure they are ready to venture into new fields and move into the unknown. But their risk-taking is always driven by a clear vision of purpose and always disciplined by the evidence of an unmet need.

The Dimensions of a World Parish

The apostle Paul is a leader because he is a risk-taker driven by the vision of taking the name of Christ into uncharted territory and disciplined by the evidence of unmet need. If he had lived in the time of the automobile, he might have displayed the bumper sticker that reads, "Think globally; act locally." Both local and global dimensions define Paul's world parish. One dimension is within the walls of Jerusalem, home base for Jewish Christians. The other dimension stretches to the borders of Illyricum on the outer limits of the known world. In counterbalance, then, the "spiritual space" for which he assumes responsibility includes both unevangelized territory abroad and unmet needs at home. Paul confirms this concept of spiritual space when he says that he wants to make a rest stop at Rome on his way to the unevangelized territory of Spain. First, however, he says that he must go to Jerusalem with an offering from the Gentile churches in Macedonia and Achaia for the poverty-stricken Jewish Christians in the Holy City. By asking for their prayers for protection as he goes home to Jerusalem, Paul reminds us that the risks of meeting human need at home are just as hazardous as the threats of death on a distant field.

So, when Paul says that he will not preach where others have preached, he does not limit his territory to the uncharted territory of regions beyond but includes the unmet human needs in the spiritual space called "home."

As chair for the Research and Development Committee for the United Way of the Bluegrass in Lexington, Kentucky, I led a study of family abuse for the region. The findings showed that 1 out of 10 homes in our community was a place of physical violence. We were surprised to find that abuse proved to be no respecter of class, color, age, or sex. The shock came when the study also showed that creed made no difference. Violence was just as prevalent in the homes of church-related families as in nonchurch families. Immediately, we called the clergy together with an urgent plea to revise their assumptions about family violence and respond with ministries of hot lines, emergency housing, and caretaking services for spouses and children.

Priorities in a World Parish

With a similar motive in mind, Paul explains to the Romans why he has not come to visit them. His first task is to saturate the space that God has entrusted to him at home and make sure that the churches he founded are solid before moving on. At the same time, he will not build on another man's foundation. Can you imagine Paul's rage if he were witness to the competition, imitation, and duplication among churches today? He would bring back Isaiah's prophecy as the motive for our witness, "They who had no news of him shall see, and they who never heard of him shall understand" (Rom. 15:21, NEB).

We cannot forget that Paul's intensity made him a slave to his ambition. When F. F. Bruce wanted to find words to sum up his biography of the man and his message, he chose the title *Paul: The Apostle of the Heart Set Free*. Out on the frontier of physical space where the very name of Christ had not been heard or on the frontier of human space where the redemption of Christ had not been received, Paul preached Christ with the exuberance of a heart set free. To hear the hymns and read the message of the Wesleys, we feel the same spirit. Our world parish vibrates with the sounds of freedom.

As Wesleyans, we get the message. Nothing more needs to be said. We now understand what Jesus means when He tells His disciples, "Let us move on" (NEB). We know why Paul said, "I will not preach where others have preached" (paraphrased). We see through Wesley's eyes when he looked out and claimed "all the world as my parish." We accept Graham's explanation when he answers thousands of invitations with the simple explanation, "I cannot come." To speak the meaning of free and full grace in a world parish is our commission, to glorify Christ with the authority of compassion is our example, and to announce Christ as the ultimate hope for the heart set free is our goal.

Our 21st-Century World Parish

Our vision of a world parish takes on new meaning in the 21st century. In past eras, Wesleyans have moved as evangelists and missionaries from the security and stature of a home base into uncharted territories. Wesley, for instance, rode on horseback over 250,000 miles around England from his home in London. Later, he commissioned missionaries from Mother England to go to colonists and natives of the New World and "offer them Christ." In turn, Francis Asbury moved from the stability of the colonies along the East Coast into the Western wilderness and traveled more than 270,000 miles on horseback back and forth across the Appalachian mountains. Still later, when Methodism was firmly established in England and America, missionaries were sent overseas to fulfill the vision of a world parish.

As glorious as our past history of missionary ventures may be, we must confess that our spiritual fathers were working on the assumption of a divided world, part Christian and part pagan. Also, their vision of the world looked like a Mercator map on which the home nation looms large while the rest of the world diminishes with distance.

Our view of the world must change in the 21st century. *We can no longer rest in the luxury of a culture undergirded by the moral concepts of our Christian faith.* To assume that the United States is a "Christian nation" is a notion that will either make us complacent or militant. Although there is still the residual evidence of a Christian culture in the United States, secular attitudes dominate us, selfish motives drive us, and sinful actions define us. One symbol of this change is the fish logo on the back of automobiles, which is a common sign that the driver is a Christian. At any urban stop street, however, you can see an equal number of cars with the body of the fish filled in with the letters spelling "DARWIN." While the antagonism has not yet resulted in a backlash of open hostility against Christians, spiritual warfare is a reality.

Racial, ethnic, economic, and religious diversity in the 21st century will further change the character of our global parish. As the United States can no longer claim to be a Christian nation in attitudes, motives, and actions, we can no longer claim what is called a "Christian hegemony" in faith. Go to any secular bookstore, for instance, and notice the size of the sections labeled New Age or Eastern Religions. In most cases, they equal the size of the sections marked Religion, which includes Bibles and Christian books. Or step outside the door of our condominium in Seattle on the way to church on Sunday morning. Yuppies jam the sidewalks on the way to coffeehouses, Sunday brunches, and body-building salons. Mixed with them are Asian couples of Hindu or Buddhist background and Middle Easterners of Islamic origin. Down the street a thin stream of white people are filing into a Presbyterian church, seemingly out of step with the flow of the masses on the hill. Colors blend, cultures mix, and creeds clash in our urban world. Having moved here from the Bible Belt of Kentucky, I know that this isn't the current pattern across the States, but I do know that every expert of demographics is predicting that this is the dominant picture of our nation in the 21st century.

How do we witness in this changing global parish? Certainly, Paul's working principles will not change. We must still be compelled by conviction, commissioned by grace, authorized by experience and disciplined by need as we follow the strategy of the Holy Spirit into that world. But our outlook must change. *First, we must recognize that every nation is a mission field.* To divide the world into home and foreign fields or into local church and global ministries is no longer real nor right. With this division comes the superior attitude of which Christians have been accused by critics of world missions. Although the criticism is unfair, we must confess the tendency to see ourselves as the majority addressing the minority, the educated teaching the ignorant, the cultured tolerating the uncouth, the rich giving to the poor, and the Christian helping the heathen. As brutal as this may sound, it is confirmed in the world assemblies of our churches. By fact or inference, white Westerners still tend to dominate the leadership, determine the agenda, and are solicitous of their non-Western brothers and sisters. Even the code word of "contextualization" in which we present the gospel in the context of the culture has a superior ring to it.

Our world parish in the 21st century will dispel that divided world, and with it will go every shred of our superiority. Leading the way is the indisputable fact that the Lord has chosen the underdeveloped nations south of the equator as the place where His Spirit is being poured out on all flesh. In the West we pray for spiritual awakening; in the South they are experiencing it. The East and the Far East are not far behind. Revivals have come to Russia and China while we await the evidence that will change our nation.

Putting these facts together, North America is as much a mission field as any nation in the world. Contextualization and cross-culture ministries are no longer concepts that we learn to apply overseas. In our changing world parish, they are essential tools of our witness to a neighbor across the street or a native across the world.

If every nation is a mission field, another mind-changing fact comes forward. *Second, we must equip every congregation to be a sending society.* Few churches in the United States see themselves as mission outposts in a pagan society. We leave that definition to institutionalized missions in urban, rural, and ethnic ghettos. No more. When we shape the definition of a mature church in the 21st century, we must go beyond the worthy goals of a soul-winning church, a disciple-making ministry, and even a church-planting congregation. We must begin to think about becoming a sending church. Nothing is wrong with the other goals, except that they tend to be geared to a homogeneous culture of persons who have some background in the faith and are socially compatible with us. A "sending church" implies a heterogeneous culture among persons who are ignorant of the faith and whose social differences make us uncomfortable.

Again, overseas congregations where the Spirit of God has graciously moved in spiritual awakening have become models for sending churches. Thrilling stories abound about newly formed churches with limited resources catching the spirit of sending their members across cultural and national boundaries as a part of their growth. In fact, for many of them, North America itself has become a mission field as they send and support clergy and laity to evangelize people who have migrated from their nation to the Western shores. From these churches, we need to learn how to enlarge our vision and equip our people in order to qualify as sending congregations ready to serve in our changing world parish.

If every nation is a mission field and every congregation is a sending society, then a third fact naturally follows: *Every member must be a missionary.* Certainly, this is not the idea of membership that most Christians in our churches have at the present time. At the least, we expect the church to serve us; and at the most, we are willing to sacrifice some discretionary time to teach a class, attend a Bible study, share a witness, or take a missions trip. If every member becomes a missionary, however, all of these dimensions change. Simply make a list of the expectations that we have for our missionaries, and we will see the radical change in expectations for church members. We would expect our people to see themselves in full-time Christian ministry, whatever their profession might be; making sacrifices of time, money, and prestige in order to make the name of Christ known; learning how to communicate across cultural lines; demonstrating the meaning of holy living in a pagan environment; and giving themselves in love to needy people whom they do not know or understand. As radical as this may seem, it is the first step in revolutionizing the church, regaining our momentum, and revitalizing our spirit.

Wesleyans have the historical precedent to lead the way into our world parish of the 21st century. When Francis Asbury announced his decision to leave the security of a Methodist parish on the East Coast and head for the Western frontier on horseback, he was forewarned that the church would die. One protagonist said, "You will be able to put all Methodists in a corn crib." Asbury responded, "I'll show them the way." More than 270,000 miles later, the West was won and the influence of his ministry was so profound that the United States officially took on the motto, "One Nation Under God."

Once again, the challenge is out. *Will Wesleyans take the risk of showing the way of witness in our 21st-century global parish?* If so, every nation must be our mission field, every congregation must be a sending society, and every member must be a missionary.

8

Community of Memory

"Wesleyans are a people with a treasured memory of the past with the opportunity to be a major player in the spiritual history of the 21st century."

WESLEYANS HAVE A RICH LODE OF HISTORY that is still being mined. Charles Wesley, for instance, wrote over 11,000 hymns in the coded language of a composer; 3,000 of them are yet to be translated for our hymnody. Scholar after scholar can make a career out of Wesleyan history, theology, organization, and practice, yet their findings only form the base for further research. In the fields of spiritual awakening for a society or spiritual discipline for the believer, Wesleyan history has few peers. The principles of John Wesley's leadership for transforming a society and nurturing a convert are timeless. Rather than being outmoded by the speed, complexity, and contradictions of changing times, they thrive on chaos and take on new meaning in turmoil.

The 19th-century Holiness Movement inherited that same history. Its vitality along the frontiers of a developing nation and its role in the Great Awakening of the 1850s cannot be discounted. Nor can we forget its role in the Pentecostal and Evangelical movements that have risen to prominence in the 20th century. Yet, in many sectors, denominations and organizations that are identified in a Methodism or a Holiness context are struggling to find their soul for the 21st century. This is uncharacteristic of their Wesleyan ancestry and unnecessary as a spiritual condition. In fact, the new movements that seem to be leading us into the 21st century, such as megachurches, Pentecostals, and Promise Keepers, are energized by the adopted and renamed principles of Wesleyan, Methodist, and Holiness traditions.

It's time for Wesleyans to get back into the discourse and demonstration of personal and social holiness in the 21st century. As people bound together by a strong "community of memory," we have something to say and do about the direction of our Christian faith in the days ahead. With a keen sense of history, we are not condemned to repeat the problems of the past. Quite to the contrary, our history is another bit of confirming evidence that Wesleyans who embrace the tenets of personal and social holiness are a people whose time has come, again.

REDISCOVERING OUR HISTORY

A full generation ago, my wife and I took our children on a trip to discover New England roots and visit the 1962 New York World's Fair. Two exhibits remain in our memory. One is the Disney display where children of all nations sang "It's a Small, Small World." The other lasting memory is the replica of the White House library and the books that were chosen as classics for the collection. As I scanned the shelves, I spotted Timothy Smith's book *Revivalism and Social Reform*. Instantly, I sensed a meaningful connection, not only with a friend whom I knew and loved, but with a past that awakened in me a lost pride. Calling my children over to the exhibit, I showed them the book, told them about Tim, and used the book as a point of pride for them as well.

Come forward 20 years with me. I am now the new president of Asbury Theological Seminary. In one of my return visits to Spring Arbor College as a member of the Board of Trustees, I talked with Glenn White, chairman of the board and vice president of the Chrysler Corporation. As usual, we were making fatherly brag points as we talked about our children. Glenn mentioned his son, Chuck, who was completing his Ph.D. at Harvard with a dissertation on Phoebe Palmer, whom he identifies as the "Mother of the Holiness Movement." When Chuck's adviser referred him to the leading authority on 19th-century Holiness history, he named Melvin Dieter, professor of church history at Asbury Theological Seminary.

Perhaps these anecdotes from my personal history help explain why I became an enthusiastic advocate for the establishment of a Wesleyan-Holiness research center funded by the Pew Trust at Asbury under the direction of Dr. Dieter. With the same pride and joy, I applaud the Wesley Study Centers at Nazarene colleges and universities. I fully believe that Wesleyans are a people with a treasured history of the past that will make us major contributors to the spiritual history of the 21st century. Especially in a time when a secular society is denying its past and forfeiting its future by squeezing time into the "radical now," we need to recover what Robert Bellah calls our *community of memory* out of which comes a *community of discourse,* through which we see a *community of hope.*

I. A COMMUNITY OF MEMORY

A "community of memory," according to Bellah, is an antidote for the "empty self" that he found in his interviews with young adults that he summarized in his book *Habits of the Heart.* Radical individualism has no connections with the memories of the past and therefore no supporting structures of "community," no understanding of the "common good," and certainly no appreciation for the "biblical vision" that our Puritan forefathers saw. Yet without this community of memory we cannot have a community of hope. So Bellah calls upon us to rebuild on a community of memory in every sector of our society, from our families to our institutions and on into our ethnic and religious backgrounds, such as the Wesleyan-Holiness Movement.

But how do we rebuild our community of memory? Bellah's recommendations are very practical for us. First, *we need to retell our story through the lives of men and women who embody and exemplify the ideals and aspirations of the Wesleyan-Holiness Movement.* Immediately, a roll call of heroes unfolds before us—Francis Asbury, Charles Finney, Orange Scott, Phoebe Palmer, B. T. Roberts, R. Pearsall and Hannah Whitall Smith, William and Catherine Booth, Amanda B. Smith, Daniel S. Warner, A. B. Simpson, Phineas Bresee, Seth Cook Rees, Martin Wells Knapp, Charles and Lettie Cowman, and Oswald Chambers. Note that we are not referring to narrow-minded, short-sighted, and mean-spirited reactionaries who are isolated from the issues of the world but are rather referring to intelligent, visionary, and compassionate leaders who were always ahead of their time. Note, for instance, the number of women in leadership who preceded the current drive for women in ministry by at least a century. Or search through the writings of these leaders for insights on contemporary issues. How many times do scholars refer to Timothy Smith's *Revivalism and Social Reform?* How many generations have been introduced to Mrs. Cowman's book *Streams in the Desert* as a devotional guide? And how do we account for the fact that Oswald Chambers's *My Utmost for His Highest* is still a runaway best-seller in Christian bookstores? Each of these books met the criteria for a classic: universal appeal, timeless theme, matchless language, and a lasting moral. But over and above these demanding standards, their faithfulness to the message of Wesleyan-Holiness was never compromised. Our heroes and their works must never be forgotten.

Our second path for recovering a community of memory is *to remember the suffering of our history, both self-imposed and inflicted*. Every historical movement, like every family, has skeletons in its closet. Our Wesleyan-Holiness Movement is no exception. We have both received and inflicted suffering by actions and attitudes. The stereotype of "perfectionism," for instance, still haunts us. I remember lodging a complaint about the description of the 19th-century Holiness revival in the exhibits of the Billy Graham Center at Wheaton. The label of "perfectionism" tends to make a caricature of our history and perpetuates a bias against our future. Yet we also know that we are guilty of some self-inflicted wounds as well as inflicting some wounds upon others. How well I remember camp meeting sermons in which "holiness fighters" were named and condemned. Even in recent days, I heard about a seminary professor in the Reformed tradition who relished the chance to ridicule students in the class who came from Holiness churches. Intuitively, I checked him off my list of theological brothers with whom I enjoy dialogue and fellowship. I was wrong because the same professor has a book on Holiness that recognizes the experience and offers an open door for dialogue. Many of us have shown a similar attitude toward our antagonists in the faith. Rather than showing the example of perfect love and entering into dialogue with them, we stopped both our loving and our talking. Until we recall our suffering received and our suffering inflicted as part of our community of memory, we cannot make changes needed for our future.

Our third point for rebuilding our community of memory is *to restore what Bellah calls the "practices of commitment," which give spiritual, aesthetic, and ethical meaning to our movement.* What are the practices of commitment that should be preserved? It is intriguing to learn that altar services, love feasts, class meetings, testimony times, and hymn sings have been co-opted without apology by the fastest growing and most effective Evangelical churches in the nation today. Even more intriguing, they do not shy away from membership discipline with a strong system of personal accountability.

The practices of commitment against which we react or for which we apologize actually form the center of vital Christianity today. Perhaps we should ask again, "What are the practices of com-

mitment—rituals, celebrations, confessions, disciplines, and vows—
that we should retain for today and pass on to future generations?" I,
for one, would want to start with the recovery of what can be called
"The Wesleyan Questions":

- Is it your desire to flee the wrath to come?
- Do you have known sin in your life?
- Do you trust Christ, and Christ alone, for your salvation?
- Do you even now have the witness of the Spirit that you are a
  child of God?

The fourth building block in a community of memory is *supporting the practices of commitment in what Bellah calls a "second language."* As with all of us, Bellah is alarmed by the loss of a "second
language" in our moral and spiritual communication. For example,
"morals" become "values," "conviction" becomes "preference,"
"character" becomes "lifestyle," "confession" becomes "catharsis,"
"redemption" becomes "self-actualization," "sin" becomes "negative
experience," and "holiness" becomes "wholeness."

The exchange of the word "wholeness" for "holiness" illustrates
my point. "Holiness" is a strong biblical word that got narrowed into
our tradition and limited by our definition of the experience. Consequently, its use still provokes bias in some parts of our tradition. In
1987, when I addressed the World Methodist Council in Nairobi,
Kenya, I used the word straight out of its biblical and Wesleyan context as part of an address to the World Methodist Council. In the discussion that followed, the meaning of "holiness" became a stumbling block. One group reacted against it because I came from the
Holiness tradition, another group did not have the foggiest notion of
its meaning, and still others wanted to dilute it into psychological
language. This is a sad commentary on our understanding of the
Wesleyan heritage, because "holiness" is being recovered by the Roman Catholic, Reformed, and Calvinist traditions in their writing,
preaching, and conferencing just as if it were a new invention. The
fact is that we have forfeited the genius of our "second language" to
terms that are more Freudian than biblical and more reflective of the
"empty self" than the fullness of the Spirit. If the present and future
generations are to understand the meaning of our Wesleyan-Holiness heritage, the recovery and enrichment of our biblical language
may well be the starting point.

Of course, we can get stuck in a static community of memory. In
the rebuilding of our history, our heroes, our practices, and our language, we must be ready for the dynamic movement from old endings
and new beginnings. By submitting our history to the critical scrutiny

scrutiny of the God-breathed truth, we will be taught, rebuked, corrected, and trained so that our community of memory can be communicated to the coming generation and activated once again in spiritual renewal and social reform. Community, conviction, and commitment are the elements of the "binding address" that holds a culture or a cause together. Without a "binding address" the core convictions of the culture or the cause cannot be transmitted from generation to generation or become a transforming influence in its future.

II. A COMMUNITY OF DISCOURSE

One purpose for a community of memory in the Wesleyan-Holiness tradition is to participate in a community of discourse with other theological traditions and religious movements, however they may be defined, as Liberal, Mainline, Charismatic, Fundamentalist, Pentecostal, or Evangelical. Some may disagree, but there is good reason for this position. If we as Wesleyan-Holiness people are confident of our position, we can enter into discourse with other traditions and theologies as a contribution to mutual understanding without compromising our position. Of course, there is the danger of being misinterpreted by such a move, and if the media is involved, there is the double danger of being co-opted into opposite camps by the big broom of generalizations in the 30-second sound bites by which the media is known.

Discourse should begin with other Evangelicals. There is good reason for this. As Evangelicals have grown in size and visibility, calls have come for the development of an Evangelical paradigm that will define the parameters of the community and give it the binding address that is lacking. This call has come from such scholars as James Davison Hunter in his book *Evangelicalism: The Coming Generation,* and from Carl F. H. Henry and Kenneth Kantzer in their gatherings of Evangelical leaders in order to frame a set of "Evangelical Affirmatives."

Countermanding these efforts is the evidence that Evangelicals refused to be boxed—politically, economically, ethically, or theologically. One need only to recall the final conference of the Council on Biblical Inerrancy before being disbanded. Even when all of the delegates agreed on biblical inerrancy as the condition of their participation, when an issue such as abortion was discussed, they splintered on their positions. Likewise, if you ask about the conference on Evangelical Affirmatives, which was intended to regroup Evangelicals and lead them together into the future, the document has long been gathering dust.

Evangelical Christianity should not be indicted for these efforts to create an Evangelical paradigm as a moral and theological foundation for the future. The efforts are the natural result of a problem and an opportunity. The problem is identified by James Davison Hunter in his book *Evangelicalism: The Coming Generation.* Whether or not we admit it, the positions that we held and assumed in such areas as theology, morality, family, and politics in the past are slipping away in the attitudes of the younger generation. Who does not agree that Evangelicals need the sense of binding address in order to teach the ethics and transmit the energy of the movement to the next generation?

The call for an Evangelical paradigm also makes sense as an opportunity coming out of the decade of the 1980s when we were wooed by the fleeting symptoms of having an Evangelical hegemony in the culture. Created by the commercial media, led by religious Fundamentalists, and nurtured by political conservatives, the heady 15 minutes of fame promised by Thomas Wolfe lasted several years. Naturally then, we have tried to capture those moments in a definition that is large enough to embrace the theological, political, behavioral, and spiritual diversity among those who would claim the name Evangelical.

Now we know that the efforts to create an Evangelical paradigm are futile. Have we learned our lesson? Richard Mouw has suggested that Evangelicals may represent a new "cognitive majority" in theology. He comes to this opinion by noting the recruiting of Evangelicals in traditionally liberal seminaries and the rising Evangelical influence in biblical and theological scholarship. Such an assumption is dangerous for us. Evangelicals never perform well as a majority, whether cognitive or moral. If the record for trying to develop an Evangelical paradigm in theology and politics is any indication, I doubt that we will fare any better with an Evangelical paradigm for intellect.

So, rather than pursuing the futility of creating an Evangelical paradigm in which one theological position dominates or compromise dilutes the distinction of those traditions, I propose that we think toward a community of discourse in which each tradition brings the security of its strengths to the table for discussion. In Wesleyan-Holiness circles, such a proposal would represent a major departure from the past. Perhaps out of insecurity, we have separated ourselves from the community of discourse. Consequently, in the last half of the 20th century, we left the field of theology to other Evangelical traditions just as we left the field of social holiness to the liberals at the beginning of the 20th century.

No one can doubt that Evangelicalism has been dominated by an Eastern establishment out of the Calvinistic and Reformed traditions in the past 50 years. The names in the Hall of Fame of Evangelical Christianity in that period speak for themselves—Billy Graham, Carl Henry, Kenneth Kantzer, Francis Schaeffer, Harold Ockenga, Robert Cook, J. I. Packer, Frank Gaberlein, and others. Only Paul Rees, Ted Engstrom, and Sam Wolgemuth would sneak into alternate positions on this all-Evangelical team.

From this observation, I draw the conclusion that lends strong support to the Wesleyan-Holiness research centers that have been established at Asbury Theological Seminary, Nazarene Theological Seminary, and each of the Nazarene colleges and universities. Through them we will not only remember the strengths as well as the weaknesses of our tradition but also identify the contributions that we can make to a community of discourse among other traditions in Evangelical Christianity. Contrary to some opinions, this calls for a position of strength, not a posture of compromise. If we stop our research into our Wesleyan-Holiness heritage, we will trade the power of our community of memory for the narcissistic view that Gehlen has called "permanent reflection."

To create a Wesleyan-Holiness paradigm as our contribution to the community of discourse is not an easy task. Hans Kung shows us the pitfalls in his attempt to create an "ecumenical paradigm" in his book *Theology for the Third Millennium.* The components of the paradigm are almost impossibly complicated in themselves—Roman Catholic and Protestant, traditional and contemporary, Christological and ecumenical, scholarly and pastoral. To balance these components and resolve the tension between them is to come to a compromise that lacks the binding address with its core convictions, spiritual vitality, and moral energy. I doubt that anyone will be ready to give their lives for the God of Kung who is "everything to everyone."

Kenneth Vaux, in his book *Birth Ethics,* gives us another example of the complexity, yet importance, of our task. Rather than settling for the simplicity of a pro-life or pro-choice position on birth issues, he weaves the intricate strands of ecological, apocalyptic, biological, psychic, philosophical, epistemic, historical, legal, theological, and eschatological factors into a cord of birth ethics that we must respect, even if we do not agree. Not to agree, however, shifts the weight of responsibility to us. Our paradigm for both ethics and theology on birth issues must be equally thoughtful and contributive.

The same can be said for our Wesleyan-Holiness paradigm. Arbitrarily rejecting other theological paradigms or refusing to enter the discourse is scholarly default. As demonstrated in the forums that our Wesleyan-Holiness study centers have held, Calvinist and Wesleyan, liberal and conservative, charismatic and mainline scholars have been invited to critique our work and participate in the discussions. As a participant in these forums, I have seen three outcomes that prove the value of the discussions. One outcome is to see theological cobelligerents find common ground for further discussion. The second is to realize that theologians who do not agree find mutual respect for each other. But the third is most important. More often than not, theologians of other traditions tell the Wesleyan-Holiness people that they are timid about their strengths and shy about their contributions. Compared with a defensive posture in the past, these discussions are a rare show of strength, not weakness, because they are based on the assumption that we have something to contribute, not just something to protect. The Wesleyan-Holiness community will be stronger if it is a full member of the community of discourse more than a maker of a self-contained and defensive paradigm.

III. A COMMUNITY OF COOPERATION

Out of our community of memory comes another strength. Until our retreat into a defensive posture early in the 20th century, Wesleyan-Holiness leaders had been at the forefront of cooperative efforts for the advancement of the gospel. John Wesley set the stage for us with his irenic spirit. In theological controversy, ecclesiastical conflict, and social conscience, he found the way to resolve issues and cooperate with others without forfeiting his own position. We remember that he and George Whitefield almost split over the doctrine of entire sanctification, but found the way to disagree and still work together. We remember that Wesley resisted leaving the Anglican Church and founding the Methodist Episcopal Church until he had no other choice. We remember that he put aside political differences with Wilberforce in order to join the fight against human slavery.

Wesleyan-Holiness leaders in 19th-century America followed Wesley's cue. Francis Asbury did not hesitate to cooperate with other missionaries on the Western frontier for the sake of gospel. Theological differences were put aside by Calvinists and Wesleyans mid-century when the Spirit of God moved through the rising industrial cities with spiritual revival. Together, they stood against slavery in the 1860s and joined in the social compassion that led to the founding of the YMCA, YWCA, Red Cross, and United Way in the years that followed.

Illustrative of this cooperative spirit, Benjamin Titus Roberts, who founded the Free Methodist Church in 1860 after being expelled from the Methodist Episcopal Church for his stand on personal and social holiness, still became a charter member of the World Methodist Council in 1881, which invited all denominations of Wesleyan background into membership. Without fear of contradiction or compromise, Roberts knew that his church, which held strongly to its Wesleyan-Holiness roots, had something to contribute to the Methodist community and something to champion out of its heritage.

Of course, the founding of the National Holiness Association (later the Christian Holiness Association and now the Christian Holiness Partnership) represents a community of cooperation within the Holiness family. More than a century of struggles for the survival of the association doesn't mean that the cause is unworthy or lost in the 21st century. The search for identity, however, may suggest that the focus has been inward with the motive of survival rather than outward with the drive for significance.

If Wesleyans in the Holiness tradition have a fault line in the 20th century in addition to identifying with the poor as evidence of social holiness, it is the withdrawal from cooperation that would provide the resources and influence necessary for an effective voice in the emerging global community. Secular organizations have learned that mergers, along with cooperative federations, consortia, and alliances, are the only way to gather the resources required to meet the needs of the 21st-century world. Regrettably, the Wesleyan-Holiness Movement has become more fragmented, localized, and independent than ever. After an era in which Holiness denominations moved to the brink of merger, the retreat from those days has blocked out the federations and networks upon which the future depends.

We need to step back and rethink the motives that have led us to "tip the hat" in courtesy to sister denominations in the faith, but never with the vision of moving our tradition back into the center of action. As the secular world has discovered the advantages of merger and strategic alliances in order to serve the world, leaders of the Wesleyan-Holiness Movement must do the same. At the most fundamental level, it is a question of resources. In our fragmented state, our denominations and organizations are pressing to make bricks without straw. Consequently, we are absent from the media, chasing after evangelical fads, and missing our opportunities on a global scale. Let me give another example. Currently, there is an aggressive move toward leadership development as the next wave in denominational growth and world evangelization. Letters announcing new institutes, departments, and seminars for leadership development are arriving regularly on the desk. Requests are made for funding-support and participation on advisory committees. But wait. As an observer of Evangelical Christianity for half a century now, I ask myself, "Is this another fad that is fed from secular success with the hope of jump-starting the future of the faith?" As a student of leadership with some understanding of the subject from both the Christian and secular sides, I also ask myself, "Are we trying to reinvent the wheel in leadership development with our independent efforts and limited knowledge?" Worst of all, I fear that we will pass through another wave in which we sanctify secular theory with the overlay of biblical insights. Until we cooperate, we waste resources and diminish our effectiveness.

No one disputes the fact that networking is the means by which the world is embraced. National corporations are showing us the way as they gain international stature by entering into strategic alliances, even with competitors. Is this evidence once again that the children of darkness are wiser than the children of light? While secular organizations are admitting that they do not have the resources to create a global network, Wesleyan denominations are trying to do it separately and in their own way. When secular corporations are entering into strategic alliance, even with competitors, Wesleyan denominations are only tipping their hats as they pass on the same road.

A community of memory that gives strength for a community of discourse must lead to a community of cooperation. This is not an appeal for mergers that create one sizable and centralized Wesleyan-Holiness denomination. To the contrary, mergers in the secular field are designed to reduce centralization and maintain the integrity of local and regional units while garnering the cooperative resources to make those units effective. One of the most positive steps into the 21st century would be a summit meeting of Wesleyan-Holiness denominational leaders who would be empowered to discuss openly an agenda for cooperative alliances with the avowed goal of advancing the gospel worldwide and moving our tradition back into the center of Christian action.

IV. A COMMUNITY OF HOPE

In the 21st century, the Wesleyan-Holiness Movement must get not only outside itself but beyond itself. One of the fault lines that I see coming out of the dominance of Calvinistic theologies in the Evangelical movement during the past 50 years is the pessimism of its prophets. Each of us remembers Hal Lindsey's best-seller of all books in the 1970s *The Late Great Planet Earth* with its dispensational pessimism. Although his predictions did not come true, Lindsey's latest book trumpets the same theme.

Also, in the last decade of the 20th century, we have the jeremiads of such leaders of Reformed theology as Carl Henry's depressing title *Twilight of a Civilization,* followed by the deepening depression of Charles Colson's *Against the Night: Living in the Dark Ages.* Try as they might, they cannot recover the note of hope after they describe the darkness.

My bias shows when I say that because of the absence of a community of discourse among Evangelical theologians that includes Wesleyan-Holiness scholars, the leading voices of the Reformed tradition are suffering from the emotional conclusion of their theology. Although they do not go to the logical extreme of Dominion, Dispensational, and Reconstructionist theologians who also spin off from their tradition, the track is the same. Their influence is also contagious. As novels have come into popularity among Evangelicals in the late 1990s, Frank Peretti led the way with *This Present Darkness* and *Piercing the Darkness.* Tim LaHaye and Jerry Jenkins have followed with their best-selling triology *Left Behind, Soul Harvest,* and *Tribulation Force.* Some have dared to put these novels into the class of C. S. Lewis's writings. For popularity, this may be true, but not in style, content, or tone. I fear that our *Star Wars* may confuse faith with fantasy and explain away human responsibility. Evangelical Christianity is in danger of becoming a community of despair. Biased as I am, it needs the checks and balances of our Wesleyan-Holiness outlook. Our theological roots in the 18th century and our spiritual shoots in the 19th century leave no doubt that saving and sanctifying grace has both personal and social dimensions that are filled with redeeming hope.

Dare I even go so far as to say again that our Wesleyan-Holiness history reveals an outlook whose time has come? At the same time that I was perusing the tomes and fantasies on the best-selling list of Evangelical books, I was asked to review two books from our tradition. One was *The Reasonable Enthusiast: John Wesley and the Rise of Methodism* by Henry D. Rack; the other was Robert Tuttle's *The Mystical Wesley.* Although neither author spares the flaws of John Wesley, there is still more hope in their histories than in any of the best-sellers that I have read.

In 1989 at the World Congress on Evangelization in Manila, I met Peter Kuzmic, principal of the Evangelical Biblical College just outside of Belgrade, Yugoslavia. Peter's seminary is the only graduate school of theology in Eastern Europe among what were Communist nations in 1989. As a speaker in a plenary session and a leader in the theological consultation, Peter spoke the vision for regional centers located at strategic points around the world for theological research, teaching, publication, and exchange. Our minds immediately merged after I presented the proposal for a global network for Evangelical Christian scholars linked by computer information and interaction.

To illustrate his vision, Peter saw the mission of his seminary in Yugoslavia as the place of preparation for evangelists and pastors who would be ready to take the gospel into the Eastern bloc when the Iron Curtain fell. Little did he know that the field would be open within three months after his address at Lausanne II. On November 23, 1990, the Berlin Wall fell and the Iron Curtain folded as students stood on top of the barrier singing, "This is the day that the Lord has made, / Let us rejoice and be glad in it."

Two months later, in January 1991, I invited Peter to speak to the Evangelical Seminary Presidents' Fellowship in Phoenix, to brief us on the changing scene in Eastern Europe. We listened transfixed as he told of being invited to speak at the first meeting of university students on the border of Romania after the Communists were overthrown. Between 50 and 75 students were expected; almost 800 showed up. From there he went to the first Christian rally in the public square of the capital city of Romania where 200,000 people heard the gospel preached in public for the first time in 40 years. Peter's summary of these scenes will never be forgotten. When he was asked to explain his doubts about the fall of Communism in 1989 followed by the surprising collapse of the Berlin Wall, he answered, "Never put a period where God puts a comma."

What better way to sum up our Wesleyan-Holiness history and future. In progression, we can move with confidence from our community of memory to our community of discourse and on into our community of cooperation. Looking forward, we see the prospects for Wesleyans setting the tone for the future as a community of hope. On the masthead of our community should be the flag that waves the message, "Never put a period where God puts a comma."

Legacy of Leadership

"Wesleyans are a people whose leaders create organizations responsive to human needs and conducive to spiritual growth."

WESLEYANS ARE REMEMBERED AS LEADERS in the spiritual history of both England and America. John Wesley, founding father of our tradition, is readily recognized as one of the most creative and constructive leaders, not just in the field of religion, but in secular history as well.

OUR WESLEYAN LEGACY

I already mentioned that our oldest son, Douglas, is general manager for human resources and executive development at Microsoft. When he was elected as a trustee of Seattle Pacific University, he emptied my bookshelves of Wesleyan history and theology in order to ground himself in the roots of the institution. Later he called me to say, "For the first time, I understand the genius of Wesley's leadership, beginning with an understanding of the meaning of holiness." He then read me the list of his insights, which I have preserved under the title "The Wisdom of Wesley"

1. Perfect love is a present possibility.
2. Faith expresses itself through love.
3. You can have the faith of a son or daughter.
4. So much urgent work; so little time.
5. Walk humbly and expect to be surprised.
6. Grow by organizing to feel and act small.

7. Take advantage of the freedom that the church provides.
8. Learn as you go from people, books, and experience.
9. Action is required when you pull things together enough to decide.
10. Attend to the poor and the weak.
11. Persecution comes when you act decisively and things start changing.
12. Embrace all that God has arranged for you.

Each of these insights can be filled out by historical events and personal illustrations. In fact, a full course in Wesleyan Leadership could be developed around these organizing principles. To read them is to realize how much Wesleyans have to contribute to contemporary Christianity. Above all, they confirm our legacy of leadership from the founder of our movement.

OUR AMERICAN LEGACY

Wesleyans also stand in the lineage of leaders of the Great Awakenings of American history—Jonathan Edwards, Timothy Dwight, Francis Asbury, Peter Cartwright, Charles Finney, D. L. Moody, John R. Mott, E. Stanley Jones, Billy Graham, and many others. More particularly, we are heirs of the legacy of leadership left to us by the founders and fathers of our Holiness denominations—an equally long and distinguished roll of honor.

Nathan Hatch, an esteemed historian from the University of Notre Dame, puts our legacy into the title of his book *The Democratization of American Christianity.* Notably, he puts the leaders of the Holiness Movement into a common mold with those who led the Great Awakenings in American history, "They shared an ethic of unrelenting toil, a passion for expansion, a hostility to orthodox belief and style, a zeal for religious reconstruction and a systematic plan to realize their ideals."

Hatch comments about our leaders who had what he called the "power of democratic persuasion," "However diverse their theologies and church organizations, they all offered common people, especially the poor, compelling visions of individual self-respect and collective self-confidence."

Taken together, these common qualities of the leaders of Great Awakenings and the Holiness Movement give us a profile for leadership that is our American legacy. We are heirs of leaders who were first and foremost *individualists fully convinced that their message represented the "pure foundation" of the Christian faith,* even though it meant going against rigid tradition and narrow orthodoxy. Second, they were *friends of common people,* fully accessible to them, masters of communication with them, and creators of educational and leadership opportunities for them. Third, they were *entrepreneurs who excelled in innovative techniques of communication and organization,* always with a democratic spirit, but not without a structure of discipline.

With this description of leadership in mind, Hatch concludes, "The inherent power of these decentralized movements springs from their ability to communicate with people at the culture's edge and to give them a sense of personal access to knowledge, power and truth."

These leaders had a head start on the leadership strategies that we commend today. In their book *Leadership,* Warren Bennis and Burt Nanus give us four strategies for taking charge.

I. OUR LEGACY OF VISION

The first strategy is *attention through vision.* Peter Drucker defined a leader simply as a person who has followers. Followers, however, must be motivated and mobilized by a vision that engages their commitment. John R. Mott comes forward as an example of a visionary leader. At the turn of the 20th century, he coined the watchword for the Student Volunteer Movement, "To evangelize the world in this generation." Around that watchword gathered such esteemed names as Samuel Zwemer, E. Stanley Jones, and Robert Speer. They, along with Mott, are credited as leaders of the modern missions movement. Around that same watchword in 1920, 40,000 college students on 700 campuses were precommitted to world missions. Even though the goal of world evangelization was not reached in a single generation, 100 years later, in December 1990, 18,000 to 20,000 college students were mobilized on the campus of the University of Illinois at Urbana with the same motive, "To evangelize the world in our generation."

Wesleyan leaders are equally known as visionaries. John Wesley had a vision of preaching in a world parish; Francis Asbury followed the vision of evangelizing the Western frontier in America; and the Holiness Movement inherited its vision from the mandate of the founding conference of the Methodist Church in America, "To spread scriptural holiness across the land, and reform the nation." Our legacy of leadership begins with this engaging vision that will still motivate and mobilize followers in this generation.

Visioning is in vogue as we enter the 21st century. Every leader, whether of international movements, multinational denominations, or local churches, are pressed to articulate a strategic vision with the energizing and empowering influence to assure vitality and viability in the years ahead. In truth, however, more vision statements are gathering dust on the shelves of institutional archives than motivating movements today. The future will bode no better without the initiation of a biblical vision anointed by the Spirit of God which undergirds and supersedes a strategic vision created by a long-range planning process.

As a consultant to Christian colleges, churches, and other organizations, I have observed reasons why so many vision statements gather dust on the shelf. Leading the way is the fact that many vision statements are "top-down" from leaders whose individualized dream fails to capture the imagination of the people at the grass roots. John Wesley would certainly fit the category of a "top-down" leader with a personalized vision of a world parish and a hands-on administrative style through Episcopal governance. Yet, he realized his vision because of the anointing of the Spirit of God and a sensitivity to the human and spiritual needs of the people he served. Consequently, Methodism became a grassroots movement with a vision that the people owned. Moreover, I would venture to say that Wesley met the definition of a leader that Max DePree gives us in the book *Leadership Is an Art.* Although speaking as the chairman of Herman Miller Furniture, DePree's insight as a Spirit-guided man is evident when he writes, "The first responsibility of a leader is to define reality; the last responsibility is to say 'Thank you'; in between the leader must be a debtor and a servant." Wesley is known for his ability to define reality in human nature and social need in 18th-century England. The extent to which he may have said, "Thank you," to those who served with him is an unknown worthy of research. But, most of all, there is no doubt that people bought into his vision because of his self-giving role as a debtor and a servant.

Another reason for the failure of vision statements is the lack of reality regarding resources. Sooner or later, every vision statement must be translated into the resources of people, money, energy, and time to be effective. Time after time I have seen a creative vision projected along with strategic initiatives for implementation. No one, however, stops to count the cost in available resources. Consequently, a worthy vision runs aground on the rocks of inadequate resources.

Even visions that are owned by the people and implemented with adequate resources can fail. Christian organizations have a major fault line in leadership when there is no accountability for the results of visions that project numbers of converts, members, disciples and leaders for the church or the number of churches planted, ministries projected, and new fields opened. Particularly during the last decades of this century, old-line evangelism has given way to a variety of movements that have held promise of jump-starting sputtering denominations, such as church growth, church planting, megachurch models, ethnic outreach, and leadership development. In each case, initial enthusiasm is projected in visions for results, but when the movement falters, accountability for results disappears from the historical record.

Through His own leadership, Jesus addressed each of these issues. His vision to "seek and to save the lost" is a lofty ideal that could only be realized under the anointing of the Spirit of God. To define reality, however, He projected that vision into a working mission statement when He stood in the synagogue to give His inaugural address:

> The Spirit of the Lord is on me,
>> because he has anointed me
>> to preach good news to the poor.
> He has sent me to proclaim freedom for the prisoners
>> and recovery of sight for the blind,
> to release the oppressed,
>> to proclaim the year of the Lord's favor.
>> —Luke 4:18-19

Utilizing the resources of preaching the Good News, Jesus dared to announce the results for which He would be held accountable—freedom for the bound, healing for the broken, encouragement for the bruised, and sight for the blind. From the beginning to the end of His ministry, He banked the credibility of His ministry on the evidence of these outcomes.

Wesleyan leaders are men and women of vision. We dare not, however, fall into the trap of "top-down" visions that do not engage the commitment of our people, project idealistic goals without a realistic review of the resources, or set goals for which we will not be accountable. Jesus is our model.

II. Our Legacy of Communication

The second strategy Bennis and Nanus outline is *meaning through communication.* As masters of democratic persuasion, our forefathers had the gift of communication in the parlance of the people. Whitefield took the message to the fields, Asbury to the frontier, Moody to the city, and Mott to the world. The question now is, "Who will take the gospel to all people through the means of global communication?" With a few notable exceptions, Evangelical Christians abandoned the field of the media. Wesleyans, in particular, have failed to claim their heritage of being pioneers of the media through publishing and radio broadcasting. Today, we are devoid of a television presence.

A few years ago, I had the privilege of being the guest of the late Gordon Rupp for high tea in the Great Hall at Cambridge University in England. Professor Rupp was recognized as the premier historian of the 18th-century Wesleyan revival. On a dare, I asked Professor Rupp the question that historians are hesitant to answer. They are loathe to apply the findings of a past generation to the needs of the current generation. Nevertheless, I took the risk and asked the professor, "If John Wesley were alive today, would he be on television?" With the slightest hesitation, he answered, "Unquestionably."

Hatch notes that Fundamentalists and Pentecostals followed the legacy of leadership through media communication in our generation. They spoiled it, but we missed it. Somehow we must recover the legacy that lets us communicate the meaning of the Wesleyan message through the media.

Earlier, we referred to Howard Gardner's book *Leading Minds: The Anatomy of Paradox*. He confirms the fact that the most effective leaders are storytellers and symbol-makers. In the short biographies of such notables as Margaret Mead, Martin Luther King, Mahatma Gandhi, Eleanor Roosevelt, and Pope John XXIII, he notes the genius that each of them had for communicating to the masses with simplicity even though they struggled with the complexity of paradox in private. When speaking to their colleagues, they could talk of complexity, but when addressing their followers, their message was so simple that a child could understand. Martin Luther King illustrates the point. When he stood before the thousands who concluded their Freedom March at the Washington Monument, King began reading from a prepared text that threatened to have him droning on and on. Sensing that he was missing his people, he threw aside the text, looked upward, and cried, "I have a dream." Today, his words are recorded in the annals of history as one of the most effective speeches ever given. With simplicity, he told a story that every child could understand.

Once in the public arena, Gardner notes that the symbols of leadership are as important as their story. Each of the leading minds whom he studied were models of their message as well as masters of language. As masters of language, they either possessed or developed the gift of storytelling. As models of their message, they embodied their story through the traits of their character. It comes as no surprise that the most effective leader has fusion between message and model, an artistic balance as the one we see when we cannot tell the difference between the dance and the dancer, the painting and the artist, or the Word and the preacher.

John Wesley qualifies as a leading mind at each of these points. Whether speaking of theological complexity with simplicity or modeling the message through the quality of his character, he leaves us the invaluable legacy of meaning through communication.

III. OUR LEGACY OF TRUST

The third leadership strategy for taking charge is *trust through positioning*. If you read the biographies of the leaders who preceded us, they are models of consistency in their positions and examples of integrity in their character. They were not perfect, and they would be soundly and roundly criticized. But they held their course and gained the trust of the their people.

In 1976, a Billy Graham Crusade was the inaugural event for the Kingdom in Seattle, Washington. On the morning of the opening rally, Billy Graham held his usual press conference. Later that morning, I picked up his wife, Ruth Graham, from their hotel to speak to the students of Seattle Pacific University. When Mrs. Graham got in the car, she sighed and said, "Billy is up in the room, totally depressed. I have never seen him so low. For more than 30 years he has held press conferences, but none like the one this morning. The religion editor of a local newspaper attacked him bitterly, and nothing that Billy could say or do made a difference. Always before, he has been able to get a fair hearing from the press even if they didn't agree with him."

Still later in the day, I chanced to meet a woman who was the social issues editor for the same newspaper and a graduate of Seattle Pacific University. Without knowing about my conversation with Mrs. Graham, she told me about going into the city room of the newspaper to write her article for the next day's paper. She passed the desk of the religion editor who was growling at his typewriter, ripping out sheet after sheet of paper, and throwing them into a pile on the floor. "What's wrong?" she asked. Through gritted teeth, the religion editor snarled, "That Billy Graham. Whatever else you can say, the man is genuine."

When his article appeared in the paper the next morning, he was still critical of Billy Graham and the crusade, but his conclusion echoed the same words that he had spoken the day before, "Whatever else you say, Billy Graham is genuine."

His words speak volumes. In the past, the worst the world could do with Evangelical Christian leaders was to have Sinclair Lewis write the novel *Elmer Gantry*. Today we have the graphic and realistic portrayal of televangelists in shackles or in tears on headline news. Through a person such as Billy Graham, we have our inheritance of leaders who win trust through their consistency and their integrity.

In our own tradition, we have a giant of the faith in the person of E. Stanley Jones. Although he is frequently misunderstood and misinterpreted, every Wesleyan should read his autobiography, *Song of Ascents*. No doubt would remain about his faithfulness to the biblical, Wesleyan, and Holiness message. In *Song of Ascents,* he tells the story of heading for the United Methodist General Conference in 1928 on a route that took him through Jerusalem. On the Mount of Olives, he wanted to pick a rose of Sharon to press into his Bible as a memory of the beauty of Christ, but an inner voice told him to take a piece of a thornbush, symbolizing the Cross, instead. When he arrived at the General Conference, he began to get votes for bishop, but he withdrew his name saying that he was called to be a missionary and an evangelist. When the vote for bishop deadlocked between two candidates, someone moved that E. Stanley Jones be elected. He started to stand and withdraw his name again, but the inner voice spoke again, "Don't touch it." Consequently, he was elected to cheers and applause. But during the night he tossed and turned until he knew that he had to resign.

The next day, the pressure mounted as he was told that he couldn't reject the call of the church. Totally frustrated, Jones went through the practice of the consecration service and took his place on the platform with the bishops, feeling out of place and confused. The inner voice then said, "Now is the time." He went to the presiding officer and asked for a point of privilege. Thanking the conference for the honor bestowed upon him, he repeated his vow, "But I am called to be a missionary and an evangelist, I hereby submit my resignation." Some said that he shot the episcopacy full of holes. Jones simply said that he got back on track. His skies were clear that night, and when he looked into his Bible the next morning he saw the thornbush had bloomed as the rose of Sharon.

Even more important, another bishop told him. "When it appeared as if you buckled under the pressure, I said, guidance is bunk. But when you arose to resign and confirmed your calling as a missionary and an evangelist, my faith came back. You didn't know it, but my spiritual life was in your hands at that moment."

This is the legacy of trust through positioning that we, as Wesleyans and leaders, must claim and continue.

IV. OUR LEGACY OF SACRIFICE

The fourth strategy we find in *Leadership* is *empowerment through self-deployment.* Behind this strategy is the principle that leaders set the tone and determine the response of their followers. If we want to empower people, we must sacrificially give ourselves away.

Francis Asbury is a prime example of this quality in our legacy of leadership. He is an exception to Hatch's description of Wesleyan and Methodist leaders because he retained an episcopal structure and an authoritarian style in his ministry along the Western frontier on the bridge of time between the 18th and 19th centuries. Yet, through that structure and style he gave himself so sacrificially to the common people that Methodism became a dominant moral force along the Western frontier on the momentum of his ministry. How can we account for this apparent contradiction? In *The Democratization of American Christianity,* Hatch writes:

> Asbury's life is a heroic testament . . . [He] introduced Methodism to thousands of young itinerants during his thirty-one years as a bishop. Yet he never asked a preacher to endure a hardship that he did not undertake regularly . . . he never found time to marry, build a home, or to accumulate possessions beyond what a horse could carry. He shared the same subsistence allotment from the churches as any Methodist itinerant. [His] circuit averages five thousand miles annually and took him across the Alleghenies sixty-two different times. He preached daily, slept in the crudest of hovels, maintained a massive correspondence and was responsible for an entire army of itinerants—some seven hundred strong at the time of his death.

Hatch continues that when a critic compared Asbury to the pope, he answered:

> For myself, I pity those who cannot distinguish between a Pope of Rome, and an old, worn man of about sixty years, who has the power given him of riding five thousand miles a year, at a salary of eighty dollars, through summer's heat and winter's cold, traveling in all weather, preaching in all places; his best covering from rain often but a blanket; the surest sharpener of his wit, hunger—from fasts, voluntary and involuntary; his best fare, for six months of twelve, coarse kindness; and his reward; suspicion, envy, and murmuring all the year round.

Now we know what Asbury meant when he told his colleagues in the clergy who preferred to stay behind in the comfort of the Eastern seaboard, "I'll show you the way." Through the power of sacrificial self-deployment, he led "a military mission of short-term agents" and won the wilderness.

CLAIMING OUR LEGACY

We need one more stop on our journey through the history of our leadership. George Gallup Jr. brings us home in his book titled *The People's Religion.* His survey is full of surprises about the religion of Americans in the 1990s. We are surprised to learn that

the religious beliefs of a majority of Americans as we enter the 1990s are not substantially different from our beliefs in the 1930s and 1940s;

. . . those beliefs in such fundamentals of orthodoxy as belief in God and in the afterlife are stable and enduring among us, and in addition;

. . . between the years 1978 and 1988, there were significant increases in daily Bible reading, belief in Jesus Christ as the Son of God, and a commitment to Jesus Christ based upon a personal spiritual experience.

Contrary to the doomsayers and pessimists among us, we have a religious base among the masses upon which to build in the 21st century. What do we need to do? Gallup also gives us the expectations of the American people for the church and its ministries:

1. We must communicate with our people in order to make their faith meaningful in their lives.
2. We must have greater concentration upon religion itself, namely the resources for spirituality in depth.
3. We must get involved in community concerns because this is where our people are having to test their faith.
4. We must get young people into the churches or else suffer the loss of another generation.

Gallup's observations have the certain sound of our Wesleyan heritage. Once again, it is the common people and the coming generation with whom we must communicate a meaningful message of spiritual depth and social concern demonstrated through our self-sacrifice.

Despite the signs of hope that Gallup sees for our Christian faith in this generation, he also flies some flags of storm warnings, which he identifies as critical "gaps" in American religion:

1. The "Ethics" gap between our beliefs and our practices;
2. The "Knowledge" gap between our experience and our faith;
3. The "Belonging" gap between church and millions of believers who belong to no congregation.

Each of these gaps is both a threat and an opportunity for our Wesleyan witness. The ethics gap threatens the integrity of personal and social holiness but opens up the opportunity to bring them together again in the experience of entire sanctification. The knowledge gap threatens the identity of Wesleyans as "reasonable enthusiasts, but invites us to take leadership for uniting faith, learning, and living." The belonging gap threatens the livelihood of Wesleyan denominations but calls out the urgency of demonstrating the biblical meaning of the Body of Christ in the setting of the redemptive community.

In reflective moments, I have asked myself, "How would John Wesley respond to the religious trends that are driving forces for the 21st century?" One of those trends is the religious pluralism that shows Muslims, Hindus, Buddhists, and Sikhs among the fastest growing groups in the United States. Another is the rise of cultic groups led by Mormons and Jehovah's Witnesses who are growing rapidly by aggressive evangelism. Still another trend is the Pentecostal movement with millions of adherents and converts focusing spirituality on emotional and ecstatic experiences. Megachurches also represent a trend with which we must cope. Recognized as one of the most significant developments among social institutions in the latter half of the 20th century, their rejection of traditional denominationalism and clerical authority combined with generic evangelical theology and "seeker-sensitive" worship packaged for consumer tastes certainly tests our tradition. Last of all, the quest for spirituality among all generations, races, and classes is a threat to narrow definitions of sanctification but an opportunity for Wesleyans to demonstrate the beauty of holiness in life and love.

Risking the thought of putting myself into John Wesley's mind, I believe that he would: (1) welcome religious pluralism as a ministry opportunity in his world parish; (2) continue to creatively develop structural forms that followed the functions that served human need and nurtured spiritual growth; (3) applaud the megachurch, which provided for both corporate worship and small-group ministries; (4) contend vigorously for the biblical authority of the clergy; (5) reject wholeheartedly generic theology; and (6) urge Wesleyans to leap forward as examples of true spirituality by holy living and sacrificial love.

Permit me, then, to add the Wesleyan movement to Hatch's concluding sentence as the challenge to our leadership in the 21st century: "American Christianity and the Wesleyan Movement must continue to be powered by ordinary people and by the contagious spirit of the efforts to storm heaven by the back door."

Our legacy is clear, and our hour has come. The Wesleyan movement is still the people's religion. If we are to claim our legacy of leadership for the 21st century, we must once again "storm heaven by the back door."

10 ═══
Timeless Hope

"Wesleyans are a people of hope, thoroughly realistic about human sin, but joyously optimistic about God's grace."

NO TRAGEDY IS GREATER THAN THE FALL OF THE MIGHTY! Isaiah, in his prophecy, weeps over the downfall of the children of Israel in the 6th century B.C. Although they had been chosen by God to be His servants bringing the light of salvation to all the earth, their rebellion took them to the disgrace of exile in pagan Babylon. Their bondage was aggravated by the fact that they were demeaned as a nation and derided as a people. As generation after generation passed in the years of exile, the pagan influence of Babylon took its toll. Some Jews prospered as merchants, others served as slaves, but almost all had forsaken their spiritual heritage. Only a remnant kept God's promise alive by telling and retelling the story of the Exodus from the land of Egypt and reminding each generation of the servant role in human redemption. In the story was the promise that God would lead them back to Jerusalem where they would rebuild the Holy City and its Temple as world-recognized symbols of His salvation. Still, they despaired of their future. Babylon ruled the earth, and Jerusalem languished under rubble. To think of being freed to make a 700-mile trek across the treacherous desert and mountain wilderness was insanity. God had forgotten them. Why should they remember Him?

Into their despair comes the prophetic promise of God, spoken directly by Isaiah:

Forget the former things;
   do not dwell on the past.
See, I am doing a new thing!
   Now it springs up; do you not perceive it?
I am making a way in the desert
   and streams in the wasteland.
                         —Isa. 43:18-19

HISTORY REPEATS ITSELF

Wesleyans of the 21st century may readily identify with the Israelites of the 6th century B.C. Both can look back to a past when they moved the world from the place they stood. The children of Israel can remember the glory of the Kingdom during David's day when the Holy City and its Temple had a worldwide influence. Wesleyans can recall the history of revival in 18th-century England when the nation was transformed under the movement of the Holy Spirit.

Israelites of the 6th century B.C. and Wesleyans of the 21st century A.D. also know what it means to be exiled in a strange land. Whether Israelites in pagan Babylon who saw a pagan idol on every corner or Wesleyans in secular America who see a materialistic symbol in every ad, their spiritual exile is similar. They may see their numbers declining, their identity fading, their competition rising, their members divided, their young defecting, and worst of all, their hopes diminishing. Both may wonder whether God has forgotten them. Both may doubt that they will ever leave their exile. At best, with 2,600 years between their generations, Wesleyans of the 21st century and Israelites of the 6th century before Christ can only cling to the promise that God has created, chosen, called, and covenanted with them to be His servants for the salvation of the earth.

The promise for the Israelites in Babylonian bondage was the story of their Exodus from Egypt when God miraculously delivered them from slavery, led them through the wilderness, and brought them into the Promised Land. The promise for 21st-century Wesleyans is found in our stories of John and Charles Wesley leading a revival that saved England from revolution and Francis Asbury's circuit riders bringing the gospel to the frontier and saving our fledging nation from bloody hostility between the East and the West.

As glorious as the past of Israel may have been, God sent the bold word through His prophet Isaiah, "Forget the former things; do not dwell on the past. See, I am doing a new thing! Now it springs up; do you not perceive it?" (Isa. 43:18-19). After the announcement of this bright promise, all of the remaining chapters of Isaiah's prophecy tell the story of "new" things. There are such immediate themes as the children of Israel returning from Babylon to rebuild the Temple and making Jerusalem again the Holy City for Jews in every corner of the earth. There are also the futuristic themes of peace for all nations and the restoration of all creation in a new heaven and a new earth. All of these promises, however, turn upon the grandest theme of all, the coming of God's Servant to bring salvation to all people. In that promise, God will give them a new story to tell, a new song to sing, and a new sight to see.

God's promise to the Israelites at the end of the 6th century B.C. still holds for us today. When dispirited or doubtful, He enlivens us with the word of hope, *"See, I am doing a new thing!* Now it springs up; do you not perceive it?" For Wesleyans at the beginning of the 21st century A.D., He has a new story for us to tell, a new song for us to sing, and a new sight for us to see.

I. A New Story to Tell

Jewish people are known for their stories. When a Jewish child asked a question, the father invariably answered, "Let me tell you a story."

My wife, Janet, and I visited the museum in Jerusalem where the Dead Sea Scrolls are on display. One room in the museum houses a mock-up model of Masada, the fortress high above the western shore of the Dead Sea where 960 Jews died rather than surrender to the Roman army in A.D. 66. Twenty-five or 30 Jewish schoolchildren sat cross-legged on the floor as the teacher told them the story of Masada, using the scale model as her visual aid. We stopped our tour in order to become her students as she gave this epic account of courage and faith with the touch of an artist and the flair of a dramatist. When she finished, in the hush of the room, she silently scanned every face in her class and then solemnly said, "Remember who are you. You are a Jew."

As powerful as that story may be, no Jewish legend supersedes the story of the Exodus from Egypt. Time and time again in the Old Testament God calls His people to "remember" the Exodus and know that they are the people of His creation, His choice, His calling, and His covenant. But now, when the Israelites of the 6th century are exiled in Babylon, God tells them that He will give them a new story that is all their own.

Each of us needs our own story. While statistics can tell "What?" we are, only our unique story can tell "Who?" we are. Statistically, I am David McKenna, 5'10" in height, 182 pounds in weight, and 69 years of age with a cholesterol count of 210. But to know "Who?" I am, you must hear my story.

Craig Dystra in *Vision and Character* says that stories are natural to Christians because of God's continuing acts of redemption in the world. When we hear the stories of God's saving acts we know that He has not forgotten us and that He is still at work in the world. For these reasons, God gives the children of Israel in exile a new story that is all their own. In the story of the Exodus, He delivered Israel from Egyptian bondage by parting the Red Sea, leading His people across on dry ground, and closing the waters to swamp the horses and chariots of the pursuing army. Now, He promises a new exodus. God says, "I am making a way in the desert and streams in the wasteland" (Isa. 43:19). In the old Exodus, He turned the water into dry land; in the new exodus, He says that He will turn the dry land into water. In the old Exodus, He guided the children of Israel by smoke and fire despite their circuitous wanderings through the desert and over the mountains; in the new exodus, God says that He will personally lead their march like a "sapper" or forerunner who goes ahead of a royal procession to lower the mountains and raise the valleys in order to make the way straight. Throughout the Bible, water is the symbol of salvation, and the role of the forerunner points forward to John the Baptist preparing the way for the Christ. So, whereas the past generation of Jews had the story of the old Exodus, which established the nationhood of Israel, the new generation will have its own story, which will bring salvation for all people.

Oh, the power of a story. An African-American Baptist preacher who did his doctoral dissertation on black preaching told me about Bishop Francis Asbury having a servant who traveled with him named "Black Harry." Although Black Harry was illiterate, Asbury taught him to read and soon he learned to preach. On one occasion, Black Harry was preaching in a frontier church that was too small for the crowd. Those outside the church could hear the preacher, but they could not see his face. After the sermon was finished, one of the persons outside the church remarked, "What a sermon Bishop Asbury preached!" Someone inside the church made the correction, "That wasn't Bishop Asbury preaching. That was his servant, Black Harry." Astounded, the outsider answered, "Well, if that was the servant, what must the master be?"

What is our own story? Each of us needs the "new" and the "now" story of God's grace springing up in our lives. After all of our efforts to analyze, strategize, and standardize church growth, the secret is out. Churches grow when individuals enthusiastically tell others their own story of what God has done for them.

What will be the story for our generation of Wesleyans? Whenever I visit the World Methodist Museum in Lake Junaluska or the historical center for our Free Methodist Church, I view the exhibits with both appreciation and apprehension. I appreciate the glory of our past, but I find myself trying to visualize what pictures and stories will represent our generation. On one visit, I even imagined an exhibit section titled "The 21st-Century Wesleyan Movement." The display case was empty. With our history still to be written, what will the next generation see in that exhibit? Will they see only the nostalgic story of our glorious past, the wistful story of a stagnated movement, or the new story of God's amazing grace in our day? Which story will we write?

II. A New Song to Sing

A new song goes hand in hand with a new story. Immediately after God makes His promise of "new things," He speaks through music to His prophet Isaiah with the melodious words:

> Sing to the LORD a new song,
> his praise from the ends of the earth . . .
> Let them give glory to the LORD
> and proclaim his praise.
> —Isa. 42:10, 12

Note the nature of Israel's new song. As their new story told "Who?" they were, their new song tells "Who?" God is.

Wesleyans are known as a singing people. Our Wesleyan hymns are shared with all believers around the world. Every time I visit a non-Wesleyan church, I open the hymnal to check on Charles Wesley's contribution to their worship. More often than not, he is responsible for more hymns than any other composer. Only the new story of matchless grace could produce such songs as "O for a Thousand Tongues," "Love Divine, All Loves Excelling," or "And Can It Be?" My only regret is to hear those congregations mumble the words at a droning pace. When I was the president of Asbury Theological Seminary, I told audiences all over the world, "If I could waft you by the Spirit into our chapel service when the students are singing 'And Can It Be?' you would be an Asburian forever." Wesleyans must never lose their identity as a singing people. But wait, as rich as we are in the heritage of our hymns, does God have a new song for us to sing?

I was in Columbus, Georgia, for a Christian Leaders' Conference. At the banquet dinner on the opening night, the host, Paul Amos, chairman of the board for American Family Life Insurance, a multibillion-dollar international corporation, welcomed the 250 community leaders and their spouses with the grace of a Southern gentleman, the dignity of a corporate executive, and the spirit of a Methodist lay leader. After the welcome, he announced to his audience, "I want to sing my song." With an untutored voice, he began, "I am satisfied with Jesus. Is He satisfied with me?" Following dinner, a professional soprano sang and I gave the keynote address. I doubt that anyone remembers her song or my speech, but no one will ever forget the moment when Paul Amos sang his song.

Why does God want to give us a new song? The answer is that song best expresses our praise to God. Harry Blamires, in his book *Recovering the Christian Mind,* says that there is a limit to what we can say about being redeemed. Words such as "peace, joy, and love" soon exhaust our vocabulary. "Indeed," Blamires writes, "even the greatest of poets cannot sustain for long the verbal record of bliss." As one of those poets agreed, "A poem is never finished. It is finally abandoned in despair." Why? Because words cannot fully express the depth, height, and range of human emotion that poets feel.

Music is different. Like the multiple movements of a Beethoven symphony, our songs of praise can rise through verse after verse, telling our story, sustaining our praise, and building upon crescendo after crescendo to an exultant finale. Handel's *Messiah* is an example. Aria after aria, chorus after chorus, we are led through the redemptive story—never boring, never repetitious, never unclear. When we reach the "Hallelujah Chorus" we are convinced that our praise has brought heaven and earth together. We stand when we sing, "King of kings and Lord of lords." But then we bow in His presence as we hear the final adoration, "Worthy is the Lamb."

Oh, the power of a new song. A few years ago, the faculty of Asbury Theological Seminary was sharply divided over the founding of a new school. As the new academic year dawned, we were concerned that the issue would become personal and drive a wedge into the unity of the community. The annual faculty retreat prior to the opening of classes would be the test. We gathered under this cloud of apprehension in the setting of a Kentucky state park. After a welcome, scripture, and prayers, the evening was turned over to Dr. William Gould, professor of voice and director of the Asbury Singers. He had to be inspired by the Holy Spirit as he divided the faculty into three groups with the instruction to write the words of their own song to a familiar tune. Quite appropriately, he titled the exercise "You Ain't Heard Nothin' Yet." Obviously, this was a daring venture for the scholarly sophisticates of a theological faculty, especially in light of the conflict among them. Imagine, then, one of the groups bringing back these words to the tune "My Bonnie Lies over the Ocean."

> *There was a young lady from Hyde*
> *Who was washed out to sea with the tide.*
> *'Twas a man-eating shark,*
> *Who was heard to remark,*
> *"I knew the Lord would provide."*

Healing laughter swept through our company as we sang silly songs together. Under the power of a song, we took the first step toward the resolution of a divisive issue.

This isn't the first time that Wesleyans and Methodists have laughed at themselves. James Warren, historian of Methodist songs, recalls in his book another silly song that was sung to the tune of "O for a Thousand Tongues."

> *Well the Presbyterians and Lutherans are fine.*
> *We have a few differences, but we don't mind.*
> *Like we use grape juice and they use wine.*
> *Too bad I'm a Methodist.*

Whether silly or serious, a new song best tells a new story. After Hezekiah put his faith in God to heal him from his fatal illness and extend his life 15 more years, he gave God praise by composing his own song and putting forth the decree for his people, "We will sing with stringed instruments all the days of our lives in the temple of the LORD" (Isa. 38:20).

What is our new song for the 21st century? After reflecting upon the truth that a new story of grace produces a new song of praise, I began to listen to the new songs of our generation. I heard, "Majesty," "Our God Reigns," "Alleluia," and "Be Exalted, O God." These new songs will join the hymns of the ages because they meet the standard of Isaiah's new song. God is praised and the songs can be sung by all people to the ends of the earth. Behind these new songs of praise there have to be new stories of grace.

Wesleyans should be leading with new songs of praise because of our new stories of grace. Our movement needs a King David who was the "sweet singer of Israel" or a Charles Wesley who wrote more than 10,000 hymns. Who will it be? What will be our song? The surest sign of new vitality for Wesleyans in the 21st century will be our musical legacy for the next generation.

III. A New Sight to See

Along with a new story to tell and a new song to sing, God gives Israel a new sight to see. For the immediate future, He gives them the vision of rebuilding the Holy City of Jerusalem and its sacred Temple on Mount Zion. From every corner of the earth, then, He shows them the sign of Jews, who have been scattered to the four corners, coming home. For Jewish eyes, this would be a sight to behold, a welcome sight indeed and consistent with God's promise to His chosen people.

As glorious as this sight may seem, God has a new and larger sight in mind. He says, *"It is too small a thing for you to be my servant to restore the tribes of Jacob and bring back those of Israel I have kept. I will also make a light for the Gentiles, that you may bring my salvation to the ends of the earth"* (Isa. 49:6, emphasis added).

God specializes in lifting our sights above things that are too small for us. Yet Martin Marty reported religious trends in the 1990s moving toward personal, private, provincial, prejudiced, and particular concerns of self-interest. As ironic as it may seem, secular trends are going the opposite way. In the corporate sector, for instance, the vision of the world has been burst wide open by the sight of new global realities. Joel Barker, in his book *Future Edge,* says that the future belongs to those who are "paradigm pioneers" or people who see the world through new large and long-distance lenses. In the 1970s, Ken Olsen, past chairman of Digital Equipment, staked the future of his company upon large, mainframe computers when he said, "There is no reason for any individual to have a computer in his home." The young upstart Bill Gates countered with the words, "My vision is to see a personal computer that anyone can use in every home." We know what happened. Digital Equipment became the dinosaur of the computer world while Microsoft soared to prominence on the wings of Gates's imagination.

What is the new sight that God wants Israel to see? It is both eye-popping and mind-boggling. Imagine what it means for this nation in exile, demeaned as a worm among its powerful neighbors, to see its role as the chosen servant for God's redemption plan throughout the whole world. Imagine the close-knit Hebrew community, with its obsession for ethnic purity, opening their arms to the despised Gentiles, including their hated Babylonian captors. Imagine a small dot on the globe called Jerusalem becoming the magnet that will pull all people from all nations toward its holy mountain in order to learn the ways of the Lord. Our hindsight, of course, sees this vision realized through the coming of God's new Servant, the Messiah himself. But put yourself in the place of Israel. God's "breakout vision" would test every assumption they ever made and crush every bias they ever built. The sad part of the story is that although Israel gave birth to the Savior, the Jews themselves never got beyond the religious things that were too small for them. They failed to see the new sight of the "big picture" that God wanted them to see—being the light for the Gentiles and bringing His salvation to the ends of the earth.

What is the new sight that God wants Wesleyans to see in the 21st century? We, too, tend to get trapped in what Michael Novak called "the thick of thin things." We, too, know the temptation of paying attention to the "bigness of small things." We, too, seem willing to limit our future to the revival of our own movement. We, too, know that danger of presuppositions and prejudices narrow our vision and block our view. God has so much more for us. In the 18th century, John Wesley had the vision of a world parish. In the 19th century, Wesleyans risked their lives on the American frontier in order "to spread scriptural holiness across the land, and reform the nation." Later in that century, Wesleyans had a prominent role in the spiritual awakening that helped shape the conscience of America against human slavery and the compassion of America that is unique in human history. At the opening of the 20th century, Wesleyans had the opportunity to project their vision for the integrity of personal and social holiness at a time when the Bible was under attack and the social gospel was on the rise. At that turning point, Wesleyans withdrew from the fray and retreated into a narrow definition of personal holiness without the risk of engagement in social holiness. We needed a prophet like Isaiah who would be God's voice to say, "It is too small a thing for you" (Isa. 49:6).

How then do we look back upon the Wesleyan movement in the 20th century? Certainly, the movement has survived, but with a loss of position as a visible leader against the rising tide of the secular culture or in the surprising growth of Evangelical Christianity. Whether in church growth, media communications, book publishing, or Christian leadership in government, business, and education, Wesleyans are considered minor players. Two contrasting pictures come to mind. One is the decline of the United Methodist Church and defection from its biblical foundations, except in pockets where clergy and laity remain committed to its historic Wesleyan position and show signs of spiritual renewal. The other picture is the amazing growth of the Pentecostal and Charismatic movements, each with roots in a Wesleyan past, but now considered stepchildren of the original movement. The contrast is evident in the fact that United Methodists became identified with the issues of social holiness at the

expense of the experience of personal holiness while the Pentecostals and Charismatics fixed upon ecstatic elements of the experience of personal holiness at the expense of the issues of social holiness.

From this contrasting history, we see our Wesleyan agenda for
the 21st century. Personal and social holiness must again become
one. Although the task requires walking on a razor's edge, we have
no choice if we are to be a viable movement in the years ahead. Nor
can we forget that the razor's edge is always where the Holy Spirit
leads us and guides us. The easy way out is to emphasize one extreme or the other. To do so is to deny the very genius of the Wesleyan movement. Utter dependence upon the Holy Spirit defines our
glorious history and promises a glorious future.

Our hope rests upon two marker events in American history in
the 20th century when personal and social holiness blended together
as one spiritual force with Wesleyans in the forefront. I am referring
specifically to the revivals on Christian college campuses in 1950
and 1970. In 1950, spiritual awakenings swept over Christian college campuses. Wheaton College is often identified as the starting
point for this revival, but the evidence shows Wesleyan colleges
such as Olivet Nazarene, Greenville, Houghton, and Messiah simul-
taneously experiencing the movement of the Holy Spirit. Out of the
campus revival in 1950 came the parachurch ministries such as
Youth for Christ, Campus Crusade, Young Life, and others whose influence upon youth undoubtedly set the tone for the Evangelical
resurgence in the 1950s, 1960s, and into the 1970s. One might well
argue that these influences saved the soul of America during the political crises, social upheaval, and moral breakdown that we experienced during those years.

The second event is similar. In 1970, Christian college campuses again experienced the visitation of the Spirit. In this case, Asbury
College, a Wesleyan institution, is seen as the point of initiation in
what Robert Coleman has described as *One Divine Moment.* While
the Asbury experience is best documented, the fact is that scores of
other campuses reported a revival spirit independent of any other
school. Wesleyan colleges again were in the forefront, not because
they were favored by God, but because of a campus climate where
revival was expected and welcome. When the roll is called, Asbury
is joined by Nazarene, Free Methodist, Wesleyan, Brethren in Christ,
Christian and Missionary Alliance, and Church of God (Anderson)
schools where spontaneous revivals in 1970 are now part of their
history.

In my book *The Coming Great Awakening* I look back upon spiritual awakenings throughout American history and trace common threads that give us both perspective on the past and promise for the future. Most important among these common threads as we anticipate the 21st century is to realize that it takes a full human generation or approximately 28 years for the full impact of spiritual awakening to be realized. Applying that criterion to the campus revival of 1970, the next full generation coincides with the opening of the 21st century. With this thought in mind, my perspective of the future changes. Rather than fixing attention on the signs of moral and spiritual deterioration in the world today, I look for the signs where God is moving as spiritual awakening takes hold. I see a new sight:

- in the eyes of pastors and laypersons who tell me their stories about God's miraculous work in local churches
- in the spiritual fervor of new believers among racial, ethnic, and immigrant churches in our urban areas
- in the dialogue with college students on public and private college campuses who meet in 21st-century versions of Wesley's Holy Club to study the Word, discipline their lives, and expect an outpouring of God's Spirit
- in the spirit of millions of high school students who gather around flagpoles to pray and take oaths of purity to counter sexual promiscuity
- in the compassion of the soloist who sang the song "Daybreak" in a worship service and then was introduced by the pastor as a victim of AIDS who was giving himself in ministry to other victims in the few months that he still had to live
- in the hundred thousand men of Promise Keepers who gathered to pray at the Washington Monument
- in the struggle of a wayward nation, founded on biblical principles that cannot forsake the "true" of its moral compass, and
- in the report of a prison ministry in Medellion, Colombia, where drug lords are housed and murders were averaging one a day until 23 convicts were converted in a Bible study that now numbers over 300 participants every Friday so that the Minister of Justice now weeps, "For the first time, I have hope for Colombia"

The sights of spiritual awakening could go on and on. Wesleyans, in particular, are those who see the future through the eyes of hope.

Isaiah gives us an inspired outlook of hope for our future. As the image of God's promise that Israel will be the light of the Gentiles bringing all nations to the Holy City to learn His ways, Isaiah envisions himself standing on the eastern shore of the Mediterranean Sea looking out across the blue waters and watching the boats from distant shores racing home. Their white sails billowing in the wind remind him of the white wings of birds stretched out to ride high on the ocean breezes. In his mind's eye, he sees all nations racing home on outstretched wings to fulfill the Lord's promise.

While writing the *Communicator's Commentary* on Isaiah, I jogged every day along the bluffs overlooking Puget Sound. On one of those days, I had just written about Isaiah's image of the sailboats on the sea racing home to learn the ways of the Lord. While running along the bluff with the blue waters in my view, I was stopped by the sight of a sailboat rounding the bend. Its colorful spinnaker ballooned out front and white sails billowed behind. As I stopped to look at the magnificent sight, another sail came into view, and then one after another until the Sound was the veritable picture of white wings against the blue waters. Then I remembered, they were world-class boats racing home on the final leg of the annual regatta between Seattle and Victoria Island.

I saw in my view what Isaiah saw in his vision. Hundreds of white sails like birds winging their way home is God's picture of His promise. His redemption plan for the salvation of the world is still unfolding with this same beauty. I bowed to pray, "O Lord, never let me lose sight of this vision. Forgive me for being too small and seeing too little. Show me where You are working and help me to be Your servant in bringing salvation to all people."

Out of that same experience, I came with conviction that Wesleyans are called to be the tone-setters for biblical Christianity in the 21st century. No other theological tradition is distinguished, at one and the same time, by telling the story of transforming a nation, singing the timeless hymns of saving grace, and seeing the matchless sight of a world parish. Personalizing that distinction in the 21st century, Wesleyans will again be a people known for their enthusiastic stories of spiritual awakening and joyful songs of redeeming grace. Why not believe that God has also included us in the new sight of being the light of the world, the magnet to those who see our faith, and the network that reaches to every corner of the earth?

What will be our story as 21st-century Wesleyans? What will be our song? What will be our sight? If Wesleyans want to see the Spirit of God move among us in the 21st century, we need to ask these questions. I fully believe that we will see the "new thing" that is springing up among us even now. Will we tell it? Will we sing it? Will we see it? In His promise is our timely hope.